Needlepoint and Beyond

Needlepoint and Beyond

27 Lessons in Advanced Canvaswork

EDITH ANDERSON FEISNER

CHARLES SCRIBNER'S SONS   NEW YORK

To Him who gave me the gifts
and the strength
and to Dorothy Wittman Newton,
His instrument here,
who dwells with Him now

Library of Congress Cataloging in Publication Data

Feisner, Edith Anderson.
    Needlepoint and beyond.

    1.   Canvas embroidery.   I.   Title.
TT778.C3F433   746.44'2   79-65976
ISBN 0-684-16086-2

1 3 5 7 9 11 13 15 17 19 V/C 20 18 16 14 12 10 8 6 4 2

Printed in the United States of America

Acknowledgments

My gratitude first to all of the students and embroiderers who gave me the inspiration and the courage to take on this project. Thanks to my dear partner in both life and business, my husband, Dave, for his patience, understanding, and wonderful photographs and to Maria and Ernst who helped their mommy through it all.

Thanks to Sandy Wilkinson for her homespun yarns; Stephen Shapiro for his photo advice; the Shapiro family for the loan from their collection; the Collins family—Julie, Jim, Jamie, Juleen, and Jeremy—for their loans and for stepping in as surrogate parents when needed; Father Wayne Henry for the loan of his mosaics; and the professors at Montclair State's Fine Arts Department for their knowledge.

A special debt of gratitude to Laura, the entire Taffet family, and Father Robert Langdon for being there when so sorely needed. The Lord has created nothing as beautiful as true friends.

As the collecting of textiles and embroideries both historic and contemporary becomes more popular, the embroiderer should try to increase his knowledge of the care of these objects. Among the knowledgeable people who have helped me in my studies I extend my gratitude to Grace Wells, Suzanne Hall, and Jean du val Kane of the Valentine Museum, Richmond, Virginia; Linda Baumgarten of the Colonial Williamsburg Restoration, Williamsburg, Virginia; Susan Burrow Swan of Winterthur, Delaware; Elizabeth Ann Coleman of the Brooklyn Museum, Brooklyn, New York; the Textile Department of the Metropolitan Museum of Art, New York; Rosemary Cornelius, Ita Aber, and Jo Bucher.

Finally, I am most grateful to Elinor Parker of Scribners for giving me this chance.

Contents

Introduction

Welcome to the world of needlepoint! Needlepoint—or canvaswork or canvas embroidery, as it is also called—is the most elegant and durable of all the needle arts. In short, it is the aristocrat of the embroidery world and has been part of the needle arts for centuries. American needlepoint today is fresh and exciting. As with all forms of art, it is enjoying a revolution. Revolution brings to mind "turning around," and so we wish to turn around and take a new look at this familiar art form.

By definition, needlepoint is embroidery stitches on canvas or scrim. Investigation of that canvas backing shows us that it is woven. Textiles are usually woven, and so we will treat canvas as a textile and not limit ourselves to the traditional canvas or needlepoint stitches and techniques. Once you understand what canvas can do, almost any of the needle arts may be applied to it.

As you read, work, experiment, and try the techniques and then adapt them to your own work. See what this textile can do for you.

Canvas

Canvas or scrim is an open-woven fabric that approaches being an even-weave; that is, the distance is the same between threads horizontally and vertically. It was traditionally made from cotton, linen, or Italian hemp, but today nylon and polyester canvases are available as well. As with all woven fabrics, canvas threads are denoted as warp (the vertical threads) and weft or woof (the horizontal threads).

There are three main types of canvas: mono, penelope, and interlock.

Mono-canvas, also called uni-mesh, uni-canvas, or congress canvas, is the oldest of the canvases; it is a single-threaded canvas available in very fine meshes that are usually made from cotton or linen fibers, and comes in white or cream. Recently, however, canvas in colors has become available on a limited basis. Mono-canvas has the advantages of being softer to work with and easily manipulated in many ways, since the threads can easily be pulled out. Its disadvantages are that it pulls out of shape as you work and, being single-threaded, does not have extra strength.

Penelope, or double-threaded, canvas was developed in 1865 in France. It is also constructed from cotton or linen fibers and is available in white or cream in many mesh sizes. Within the penelope family is also cross-stitch canvas that comes with a prewoven blue warp thread usually spaced at one-inch intervals. This canvas is usually lightweight. The advantages of penelope canvas are that the double threading makes it stronger and the double threads can be split, enabling you to do two different-size stitches on the same canvas (Figure 1). Penelope canvas does not pull out of shape as badly as mono, and it can be manipulated. However, the double threads make it harder to see when stitching.

Interlock, our newest canvas, has double weft threads and single warp threads. The weaving process used for this canvas is the ancient art of twining. Interlock comes in white and clear and is made from cotton, nylon, or polyester fibers in a limited number of mesh sizes. It has the advantage of strength with easily discernible holes, and it does not pull out of shape easily. Interlock is not as versatile as mono or penelope, because its threads cannot be pulled or shredded easily.

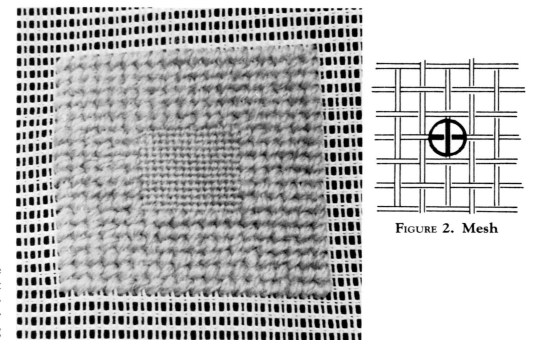

FIGURE 1. Penelope
canvas threads split
and stitched, sur-
rounded by regular
stitching

FIGURE 2. Mesh

Canvas is purchased by type (mono, penelope, interlock) and the number of meshes to the inch. Each intersection of warp and weft threads is considered a mesh (Figure 2). The mesh size is determined by the number of warp threads to an inch. With penelope canvas, each pair of threads is considered one. Mono-canvas is available in 36- and 40-inch widths and mesh sizes from 10 to 32 to the inch. Penelope canvas comes in widths from 27 inches to 60 inches and mesh sizes from 3½ to 16 to the inch. Rug-size canvases (3½, 4, 5 meshes to the inch) are also referred to as leno canvas. Interlock canvas is available in 27-inch to 40-inch widths and mesh sizes 10, 12, 13, 14, 16, and 20 (nylon). When purchasing canvas, you would ask for, say, "mono 12," which would be a mono-canvas with 12 meshes to the inch; "penelope 10/20," which is penelope canvas with 10 meshes to the inch, or "interlock 14," which is interlock canvas with 14 meshes to the inch. Novelty canvases are now also available made of such materials as plastic (Figure 3).

The quality of canvas is extremely important. The function of canvas is to serve as the foundation for our embroidery, and this foundation has to be good or our work will not last and also will be more difficult to stitch on. When checking for quality, the first thing to do is make sure the mesh is regular and not clogged with sizing. The canvas should be firm, not limp. Ideally, the fibers should be sized before the weaving so that the threads remain distinct when woven. Take one thread from the canvas and untwist it to see how many fibers make up the thread. The number of fibers within a thread is called its denier, and the higher the denier the better the quality (Figure 4). I myself never use canvas that deniers at 3 or below. When the canvas is unrolled, see that it is free of knots.

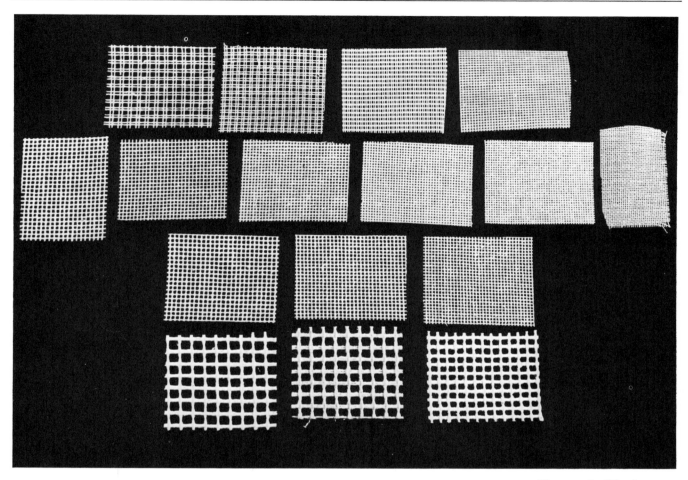

FIGURE 3. Various types of canvas in a variety of mesh sizes. *Top to bottom:* penelope, mono, interlock, leno (rug)

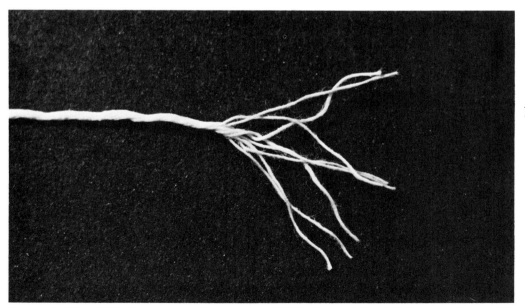

FIGURE 4. Denier 8

When cutting the canvas to the size of the design, make sure the selvedges are at the side of your work. Since canvas can shrink as it is worked, always purchase more than is needed. I usually allow a two- or three-inch border around the finished design. As you cut the canvas, follow the threads.

The size of the canvas mesh to be used will be determined by your design. When your design is drawn, decide the mesh required by laying different sizes of canvas mesh over it to see what size will give you the detail needed. The smaller the mesh size, the greater the freedom of detail.

EXERCISE

Collect various types of canvas—about a half yard of each is good. Tag each with size of mesh, type of canvas, fiber content, and the denier of each.

Tools

YARNS

The materials used in canvaswork are varied but simple. American needle-point, until recent times, has been limited to the needlepoint or tapestry wools in color ranges that can only be described as dull. Now, however, anything goes, and yarns or fibers come in a delightful range of types and colors.

Before we discuss the various types of yarns or fibers available, it might be helpful to understand the construction of what we are working with. Wools—the easiest fibers to spin—are derived from the shearing of sheep fleece. The quality of wool is determined by staple and crimp. Staple, the length of the wool fibers, can vary from 1½ to 6 inches, depending on the breed of sheep. The longer the staple, the better the wearability. Crimp is the waves or kinks in the wool fiber, and it runs vertically as well as horizontally along the fiber. Close crimp results in soft, fluffy yarn. A wavy fiber with less crimp results in a smooth, harsh yarn. Most of the Persian and tapestry yarns are spun from the long-wool breeds of sheep such as Leicester, Romney, Lincoln, and Cotswold, which provide fleece that gives a long, lustrous staple with a wide crimp.

Persian is made of a long-stapled wool fiber or thread consisting of three two-ply strands, which can be separated into three single two-ply strands. The staples or fibers are long and slightly hairy, giving excellent strength. One of the most common yarns used for needlepoint, Persian is offered in a broad color range and is moth-resistant. It can be purchased by the strand, the ounce (approximately fifty 23-inch-long strands), the hand (four ounces, approximately 200 strands), the pound (approximately 800 strands), or in skeins (8.8 yards). Persian is actually the best all-around type of wool for canvaswork, since it can be separated so that the use of many stitches achieves the same coverage on canvas.

Tapestry yarns are long-stapled wools made up of four plies tightly twisted. This is a smoother yarn than Persian and is moth-resistant. Tapestry wool is usually purchased in 10-yard skeins. This wool is useful when the stitches being used require a uniform thickness of yarn. It gives a very smooth look that is especially useful when doing Florentine work.

Crewel yarns are tightly twisted, long-stapled, springy, two-ply single strands that are quite fine. They can tend to fuzz and wear down when worked, with the exception of Medici, a very fine French crewel yarn. The advantage of using crewel yarn is that the fine single strands can be combined to assure excellent coverage no matter what stitch is used or what canvas mesh. Four strands of Medici equal one strand of Persian. The English crewel yarns are available in a much broader range of colors than the French, but the fineness of the yarn allows strands to be combined to form new shades and colors. Crewel yarn is usually sold by the ounce, but American crewels are sold on cards as well. It must be worked using shorter strands (12 to 18 inches).

Embroidery floss is a cotton mercerized yarn that contains six threads to a strand. It is extremely durable and gives a nice luster to your work. The very broad range of colors is readily available everywhere. It comes in skeins containing 8.7 yards.

Silk comes in two forms, matte and filo. Filo silk, which is used mainly for silk and gold embroidery, is very difficult to pass through canvas. It is extremely fine and expensive. I use it very sparingly and run it through beeswax as I work. Matte silk, however, works up beautifully on canvas. The range of colors is enormous, and its durability is well worth the expense. It is available in 55-yard skeins, but in recent years I have noticed some stores selling it by the strand. The matte silk strands can be separated, as can embroidery floss, with seven threads comprising one strand.

Linen threads also work up very nicely on canvas. These yarns must be worked in short strands. They come in three different weights: fine (20/2), broad, and medium (10/2); the skeins usually contain 15, 40, or 60 yards. The color range in linen is not very extensive, but it dyes beautifully.

Perle cotton is a mercerized twisted cotton with a very high sheen. It comes in several weights: #3 (thickest), #5, and #8 (thinnest). The color range is quite broad, and it is available in skeins of 16.4 yards or balls of 50 yards. This yarn cannot be separated and must be worked in shorter strands, as it tends to wear down. In my opinion, it should be used sparingly, as its durability is not great.

Matte cotton is a nonmercerized cotton yarn that has a very dull flat or matte appearance. It is available in a broad color range of 10.85-yard skeins. Matte cottons should be worked in shorter strands, because they tend to wear down and their durability is not very good.

Knitting worsted also can be used for canvaswork but must be used with care. These yarns are very short-stapled and will pill, fuzz, and wear down. Their construction also makes them very elastic so that care must be used when stitching with them. Because of their lack of wearability, they are not advised for use on objects that will receive wear. Instead, use them for such things as wall hangings. Knitting worsted is usually sold in two-ounce and four-ounce skeins in a broad range of colors.

Metallics are either pure metal or synthetic metal such as lurex, woven or twisted around a thread core usually made of silk, cotton, or nylon. These tend to ravel. The range of metallics available has become very broad. Those that are woven are easier to handle if a tight knot is put in both ends before stitching. Because metallics are so broad in range, we will discuss their uses under techniques further on.

Rug yarns come in several types: smyrna, rya, and rayon-cotton. They are heavier weights usually used on large-mesh canvas. Rya is two ply, while the others come in three and four ply. They are all rough-textured and not easily separated. Rayon-cotton fuzzes up when worked and is not very durable. These yarns are usually sold in skeins or by the pound (225 yards per pound of wool). The wool and rya yarns are long-stapled and durable.

Handspuns are now more available in stores, or you can do your own. Today there are many books on the market on handspinning, and fleece, flax, and rovings are readily obtainable in weaving supply stores. I have found, however, that actually passing or stitching with them in the traditional manner results in their wearing down and a loss of their natural beauty and texture. Couching, however, allows them to show up to their full advantage, so do very long stitches.

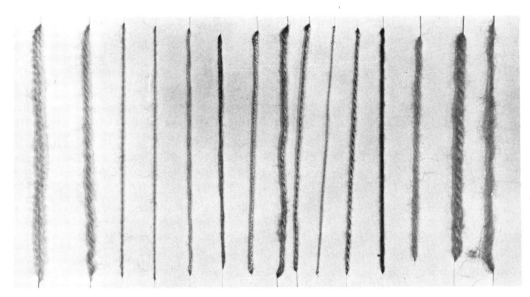

FIGURE 5. **Yarns for canvas embroidery.** *Left to right*: Persian, tapestry, crewel, Medici, embroidery floss, filo silk, matte silk, linen (heavy), linen (medium), linen (light), perle cotton, matte cotton, knitting worsted, rug yarn, handspun yarn

There are many other yarns and fibers to choose from, and experimentation with them will broaden your view of fibers for canvaswork. Among those available are raffia, rope, string, macramé cord, ribbon, velvets, and crochet cottons (Figure 5).

Yarns and fibers come in what seems to be an endless array of color. When a certain color or shade cannot be found, however, I resort to dyeing fibers. At this point, two choices are open: natural or vegetable dyes, and chemical dyes. When dyeing, I use white fibers.

There are many books giving instructions for natural dyeing that will give you the detailed procedures. A great advantage of natural dyeing is that all the colors obtained are compatible. There are absolutely no worries about color schemes with natural dyes; every color always goes with every other color. From a conservation point of view, all natural dyes are safer and will last longer than chemical dyes. As the work ages and fades, natural dyes fade but remain the same color. (Chemical dyes as they fade can change color; for example, red fades to blue-casted red.) But obtaining the intense colors of chemical dyes with natural dyes is rather difficult and the natural dyeing process is somewhat time-consuming.

Chemical dyes should be of very high quality and be used exactly according to instructions. I prefer to use cold-water dyes so that the fibers are not damaged. Also be aware that all chemical dyes are not suitable for all fibers. Silk, for instance, must be dyed with silk dyes.

Dyeing our fibers also gives us the advantage of experimentation with different dyeing techniques, such as tying sections of the yarns and dyeing only parts of the length. These procedures are a great help when you want to get natural effects such as tree bark. As you go on in your exploration of canvaswork, experiment with the marvelous effects dyeing can give.

One of the constant questions facing the novice canvasworker is how much yarn is needed. Estimating the yarn required is really quite simple. First, you must be aware of how much yarn is required to cover one square inch of canvas with the stitch you are working. Various stitches require different amounts. The stitch charts included in this book give the amounts. You can make your own estimate by stitching one square inch of the stitch desired, using a premeasured amount of yarn. Grid a piece of acetate into one-inch squares with a permanent marker; then lay it down on the design and count the number of squares that are needed for each color in the design. Multiply the number of squares for each color by the yarn required for one square inch of the stitch to be used. This result will give you the amount of yarn you will need.

When working with bargello patterns, determine how much yarn is required to cover one square inch. Determine the square inches in the entire piece by multiplying the length and width. Multiply the square inches in the entire piece by the amount of yarn required for one square inch. Divide this amount by the number of colors to be used. This figure will give the amount required for each color.

When stitching, do not use any fibers longer than about 24 inches. Certain fibers such as linen and perle cotton require much shorter lengths. As a general rule, the smaller the canvas mesh, the shorter the fiber used. Single strands should also be used shorter than the length used for three strands of fiber or wool.

As you use various stitches, you will find that certain fibers will be too thick to accomplish stitching. When working with a strand fiber such as Persian wool, embroidery floss, or silk, strands should be separated from the center out to avoid knotting and twisting up as the strands are being separated. Better coverage of canvas and a neater appearance to your stitching will result if you unstrand or separate all the strands that constitute the fiber. For example, Persian consists of three strands that should be separated into three individual strands and then recombined.

Certain wool fibers also have a direction. In other words, when you run your fingers down the fiber, one direction is rougher than the other. It is important when recombining strands that this direction remain the same. This is done so that the fibers in the strands rub each other in the same direction and give better wearability. For this reason, never fold a fiber in half and work this folded fiber as one strand.

NEEDLES

The most commonly used needle for canvaswork is a blunt needle with an elongated eye. When purchasing these needles, refer to them as "tapestry" needles.

Needles, like canvas, come in various sizes (Figure 6). The larger the tapestry needle, the smaller the number; the range is 13 through 26. As would be expected, large-mesh canvas such as 3½ to 5 would require a size 13 needle. Canvas of 7, 10, and 12 mesh uses a size 18 needle, and the finer meshes use sizes 22, 24, or 26. The needle eye is also important in determining the size to use. The wool must fit comfortably in it and not be compacted or jammed in. You should be able to thread the yarn into the eye without tremendous difficulty.

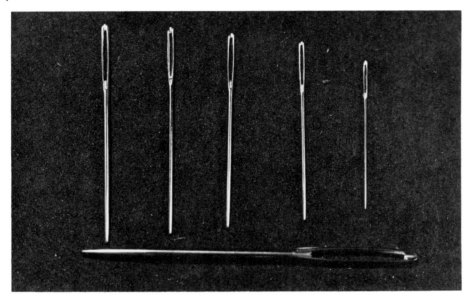

FIGURE 6. **Tapestry needles.** *Left to right:* #18, #19, #20, #26, #15

As you work, you will discover needs arising for other types of needles as well. Some useful types to have are chenille (for plunging ends to the back of your work), beading, crewel, and curved. Curved surgical needles are especially useful when working on a frame. They are available with blunt ends in a variety of sizes.

The steps for threading a needle (Figure 7) are as follows:

1. Fold the yarn over the needle.
2. Slip the needle out, holding on to the yarn loop very tightly.
3. Thread the resulting loop through the eye of the needle.

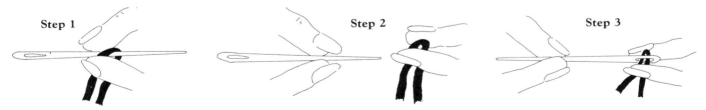

FIGURE 7. **Steps for threading a needle**

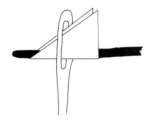

FIGURE 8. Paper-triangle method of threading a needle

Needle threaders are also very helpful, as is a small triangle fold of paper. Lay the yarn in the fold, push the point of the paper fold through the needle eye until the yarn shows that it is through also, then remove the paper so that only the yarn remains threaded in the needle (Figure 8).

More ease in stitching can easily be obtained by putting the needle in an emery pincushion periodically or running the needle through your hair as you are working.

SCISSORS

The scissors used for this work are usually fine-pointed embroidery scissors. I also have a larger, heavier pair of shears that I use for cutting canvas. It is very important that the scissors you use for your embroidery are never used on paper, as the blade edge will be destroyed. Always keep your scissors sharp and protected in a case.

FRAMES

One of the great advantages of canvaswork is that it is very easily carried about. However, there are times, whether from preference or necessity, when a frame is required to accomplish a technique. The greatest advantage to working on a frame is that your work is not pulled out of shape a great deal.

A great variety of frames is available in the marketplace, but there are some simple ones included here that you can make yourself. I personally do not recommend using a round embroidery hoop.

Scroll frames (Figure 9) are very practical and adjustable and require no lacing. They are useful for long pieces of work and also allow you to loosen and tighten the tension as you desire while stitching.

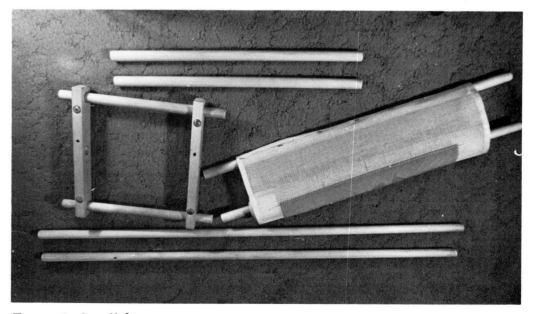

FIGURE 9. Scroll frame

Canvas stretchers, available in various sizes in art supply stores, also work very nicely. This type of frame is not adjustable in size and requires tacking down on all sides. It is, however, the easiest frame to construct. Simply put the stretcher strips together to the desired size and thumbtack (use nonrusting tacks) your canvas to it, making sure it is taut.

The canvas is taut enough on a frame when a slight "ping" sound results from tapping the canvas with your fingernail. I usually mount my canvas on a frame from the centers out to the edges for a better drum-top fit.

EXERCISES

1. Start collecting various types of yarn. Tag your skeins by type and manufacturer. Try to have various weights and sheens in your collection.
2. Tie-dye one ounce of white Persian yarn using two different colors and cold-water dyes.
3. Collect various size needles in various types. Put them on a length of felt and tag them by type and size using stick-on tags on the felt. (This can be rolled up and carried with you.)

Basic Stitching

Now that we have had a basic survey of the materials and tools with which we can work in canvas embroidery, let us start to put them to use.

To start stitching with our threaded needle, we have two basic procedures from which to choose.

I prefer the first, which is known as the waste-knot method. A knot is put on the right side of the canvas some distance away from the starting point, and the needle is brought up at the starting point. Begin stitching, but as you stitch, stitch over the thread that is on the reverse side until you reach the area where the knot is. Pull the knot up taut with your fingers and clip it off. The minute end will then disappear to the reverse side of your work (Figure 10).

The second method, which is more cumbersome, is to hold a length of the thread behind the canvas and stitch over it while you work.

As you stitch, two methods are also open to you—stab stitching or surface stitching.

In stab stitching, the needle is worked from both sides and each step of a stitch is worked up (the thread is pulled all the way up) and then down (the thread is pulled all the way down). This method is best when working on a frame.

Surface stitching utilizes the familiar up-and-down action of sewing. In other words, the up-and-down steps are combined in one step. The only easy way to use this method of stitching on a frame is to employ a curved needle. A scroll frame allows you the freedom of doing both surface and stab stitching while working on a frame by tightening and loosening the canvas on the rollers.

As you stitch, you will find your fibers twisting. Periodically, turn the canvas upside down and let the needle and fiber hang free to untwist. As you become more proficient, you will be able to untwist the fiber by rotating the needle with your fingers. It is, however, very important that the fiber be untwisted as you work, to give a consistent appearance to your work.

All things must come to an end, and so it will be with your fiber in the needle. When ending a fiber, you can run the needle through four or five threads on the reverse side of your work, either straight or diagonally. Do not dig deeply with your needle or bumps will appear in your work. Never end in the same place consistently or bumps will also appear. I find ending in a diagonal direction preferable. When pulling through to end off, do not yank the yarn too tight or the last stitch completed will not have the same tension as the previously worked stitches (Figure 11).

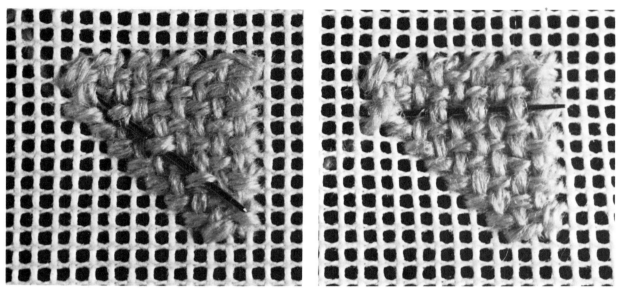

FIGURE 11. **Ending stitching diagonally and straight**

Care must be taken as you work to make sure the canvas is adequately covered. Ideally you should be able to cover black canvas with white thread and see no black. Always try your stitches on a square of canvas in varying thicknesses of the fiber you are using to see the coverage you will obtain. If, for instance, your coverage is too thick with three strands of Persian but too thin with two strands, you may have to switch to crewel yarn, which combines to a coverage in between these two thicknesses. Warm colors such as red, orange, yellow, and yellow-green appear to cover the canvas more thoroughly than cool colors, because of the dyeing processes.

As you stitch, make sure you are not pulling your fibers too tight. Tension is too tight when either the warp or weft threads of the canvas are pulled noticeably out of line. When this happens, gaps will appear between your stitching, interrupting the smooth, flowing look of your work. Conversely, stitches done too loosely do not appear defined and are lumpy.

When stitching, always work into the stitches that have been previously done. As you work into these stitches, catch just a bit of the fiber of the existing stitch to lock the stitches together. Care must be taken not to split the fiber completely; just catch a tiny portion of it. This will prevent friction between stitching from building up and destroying the fibers. As you follow the stitch directions from various sources, always try to convert them, whenever possible, to the action of working into stitching (Figure 12).

Now on to stitches to start your new vocabulary for canvaswork. I have tried to categorize the stitches included in this book into families or groups based on the actions employed to accomplish each. The families are: half cross,

FIGURE 12. Stitching into stitches and catching fiber

cross, continental, Scotch, Gobelin, brick, oblique, herringbone, bargello, star, couching, loop, and miscellaneous. On each of the following stitch charts are included the family, the number of strands used on size 10 mesh and size 12 mesh interlock canvas when using Colbert Persian wool, the yardage required to cover a square inch, notes concerning the stitch, and some suggestions for uses for the stitch. Also included, where necessary, are instructions for left-handed stitchers as well. In most cases your needle comes up on odd numbers and down on even numbers. The third row of stitching is usually the same as the first. As you study the charts, practice each one on a small doodle cloth (scrap of canvas). These can be labeled and cut apart and kept in a notebook for future reference. Try the stitches in different fibers as well. When reading the charts for stitches, please keep in mind that *threads* of the canvas are counted, not holes. Before you start, however, I wish to state that these charts are only a brief introduction to the vast vocabulary of stitches available to you.

HALF CROSS STITCH   (*Figures 13a and b*)
Three strands on 10 mesh
Two strands on 12 mesh

FAMILY: Half cross.
COVERAGE: One yard covers one square inch.
NOTES: Can be used only on interlock and penelope canvas.
    Provides minimum backing.
USES: Background, object filling, borders, outlines, shading.
LEFT HAND: Turn canvas upside down for second row.

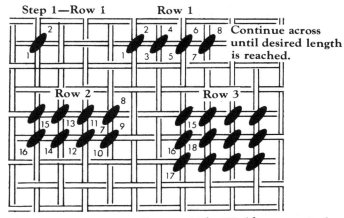

FIGURE **13b.** Half cross stitch

FIGURE **13a.** Half cross stitch

CROSS STITCH *(Figures 14a and b)*

Two strands on 10 mesh
One strand on 12 mesh

FAMILY: Cross stitch.

COVERAGE: Two yards covers one square inch.

NOTES: Crosses must all cross in the same direction.

All types of canvas may be used (on mono-canvas, each stitch must be done individually).

This is an antique stitch.

USES: Background (very slow), object filling, borders, outlines, isolated stitch, shading.

LEFT HAND: Turn canvas upside down to complete crosses.

FIGURE **14b.** Cross stitch

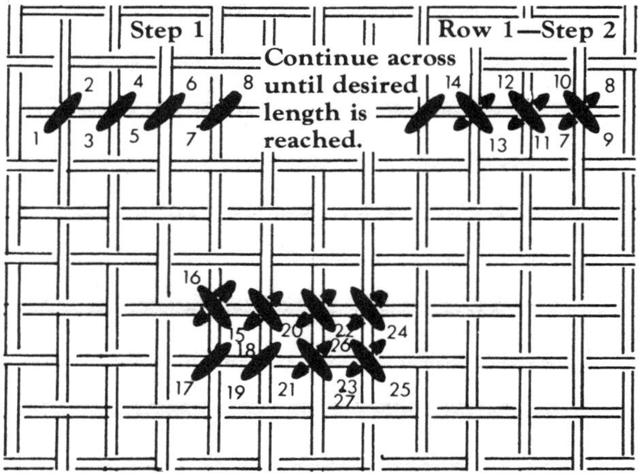

FIGURE **14a.** Cross stitch

THREE-STITCH CROSS STITCH (*Figures 15a and b*)

Two strands on 10 mesh
Two strands on 12 mesh

FAMILY: Cross stitch.
COVERAGE: Two and one-half yards covers one square inch.
NOTES: Crosses must all cross in the same direction.
    All types of canvas may be used.
    Each stitch must be done individually.
USES: Background, object filling, borders, isolated stitch.
LEFT HAND: Turn canvas upside down for steps 2 and 3.

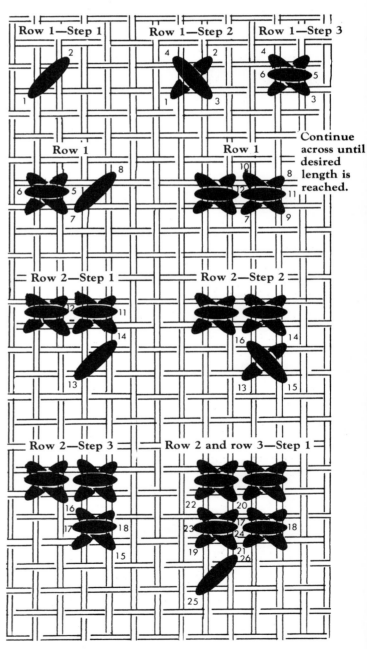

FIGURE 15a. **Three-stitch cross stitch**

FIGURE 15b. **Three-stitch cross stitch**

UPRIGHT CROSS STITCH *(Figures 16a and b)*

Two strands on 10 mesh
Two strands on 12 mesh

FAMILY: Cross stitch.
COVERAGE: Three yards covers one square inch.
NOTES: Crosses must all cross in the same direction.
    All types of canvas may be used.
USES: Background, object filling, shading.

FIGURE 16a. Upright cross stitch

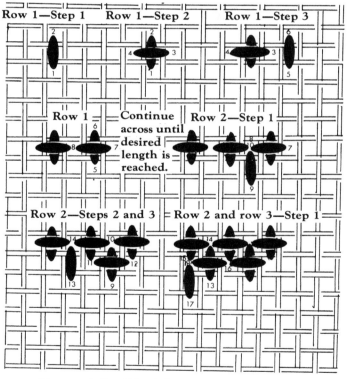

FIGURE 16b. Upright cross stitch

CONTINENTAL STITCH *(Figures 17a and b)*

Three strands on 10 mesh
Two strands on 12 mesh

FAMILY: Continental.
COVERAGE: One and one-half yards covers one square inch.
NOTES: All types of canvas may be used.
   Covers the back well.
   Pulls the canvas out of shape.
   All stitches must slant in the same direction.
USES: Background, object filling, borders, outlines, shading.

FIGURE 17a. **Continental stitch**

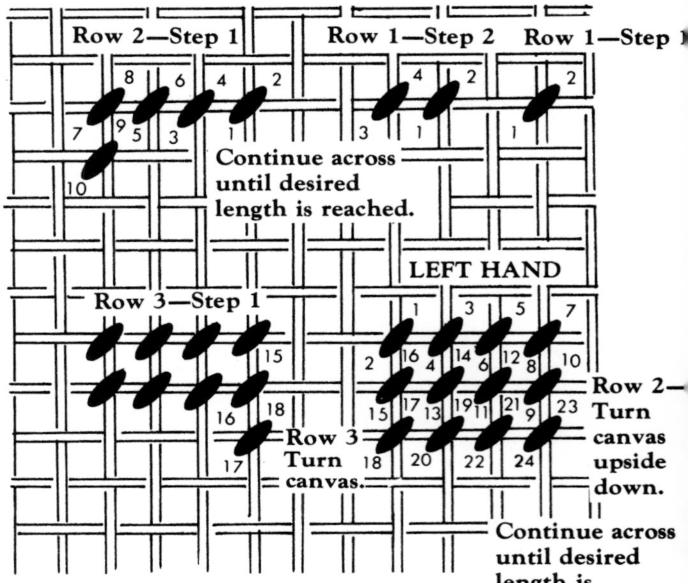

FIGURE 17b. **Continental stitch**

BASKETWEAVE STITCH *(Figures 18a and b)*

Three strands on 10 mesh
Two strands on 12 mesh

FAMILY: Continental.
COVERAGE: One and one-half yards covers one square inch.
NOTES: All types of canvas may be used.
   Covers the back well.
   Does not pull the canvas out of shape.
   All stitches must slant the same way.

Make sure stitches working from the top down are done over warp
threads that are on top.

USES: Background, object filling, shading.

FIGURE 18a. Basketweave stitch

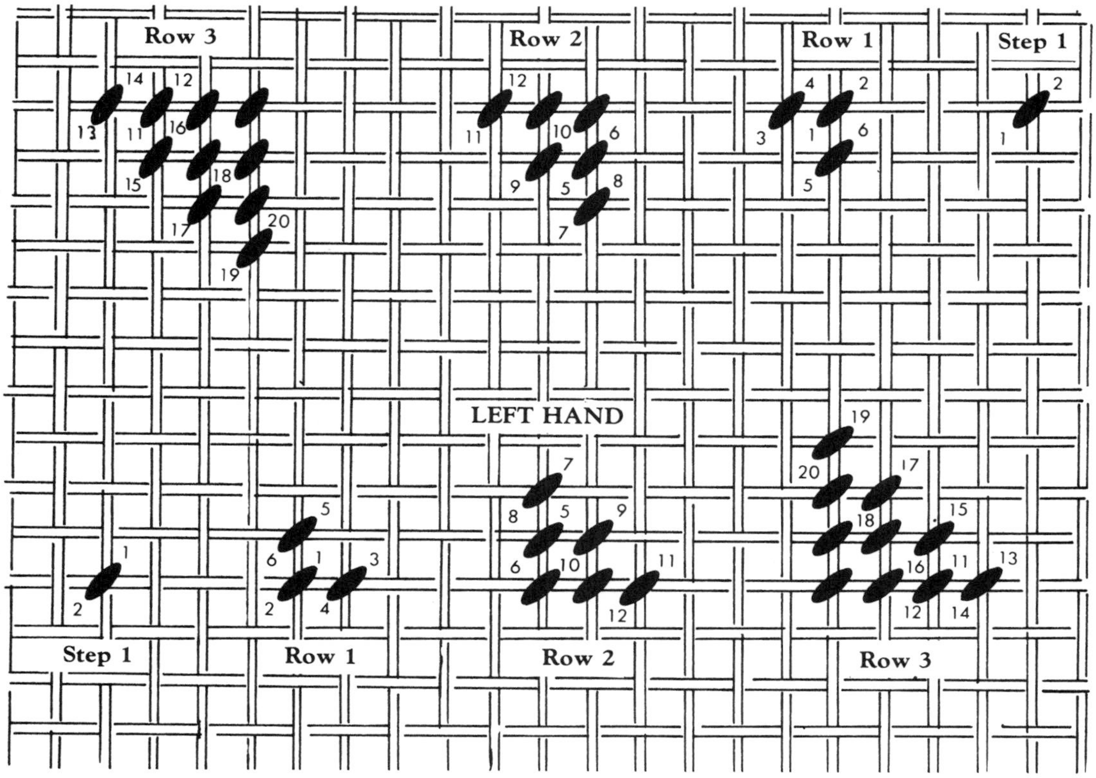

FIGURE 18b. Basketweave stitch

SCOTCH STITCH *(Figures 19a and b)*

Three strands on 10 mesh
Two strands on 12 mesh

FAMILY: Scotch.
COVERAGE: Three and one-half yards covers one square inch.
NOTES: All types of canvas may be used.
   All stitches must slant in the same direction.
   Can be enlarged or reduced.
USES: Background, object filling, border, isolated stitch.

FIGURE **19a.** Scotch stitch

FIGURE **19b.** Scotch stitch

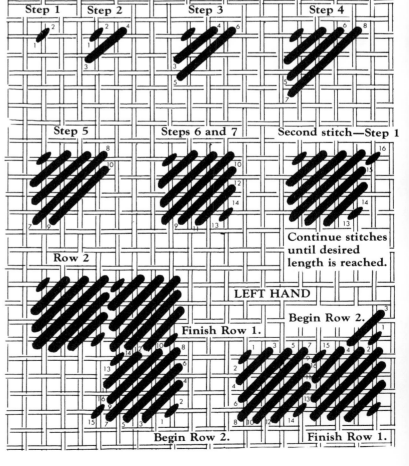

MOSAIC STITCH *(Figures 20a and b)*

Three strands on 10 mesh
Two strands on 12 mesh

FAMILY: Scotch.
COVERAGE: Two yards covers one square inch.
NOTES: All types of canvas may be used.
Stitches must all slant in the same direction.
Covers the back well.
USES: Background, object filling, border, isolated stitch.
LEFT HAND: Turn canvas upside down for second row.

FIGURE 20a. Mosaic stitch

FIGURE 20b. Mosaic stitch

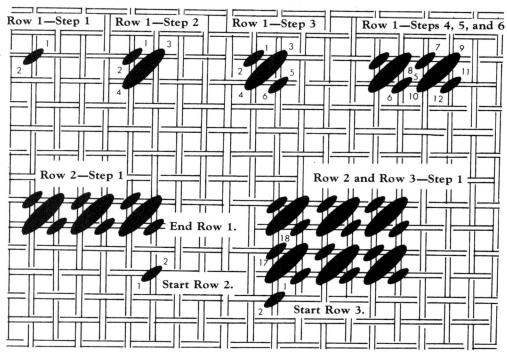

DIAGONAL MOSAIC STITCH *(Figures 21a and b)*

Three strands on 10 mesh
Two strands on 12 mesh

FAMILY: Scotch.
COVERAGE: Two yards covers one square inch.
NOTES: All types of canvas may be used.
     Stitches must all slant in the same direction.
     Covers the back well.
USES: Background, object filling.

FIGURE 21a. **Diagonal mosaic stitch**

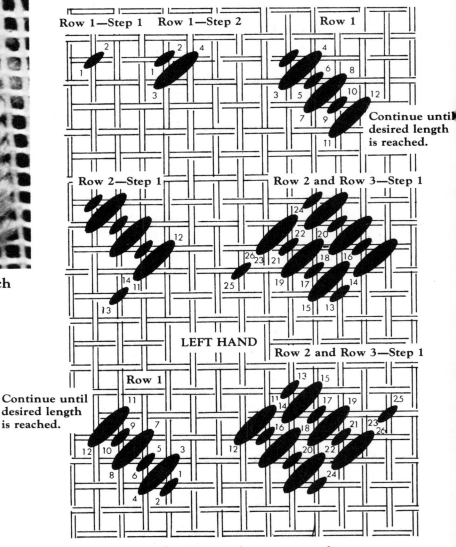

FIGURE 21b. **Diagonal mosaic stitch**

UPRIGHT GOBELIN STITCH *(Figures 22a and b)*

Three strands on 10 mesh
Two strands on 12 mesh

FAMILY: Gobelin.

COVERAGE: Two yards covers one square inch.

NOTES: All types of canvas may be used.

Covers the back well.

Can be enlarged.

Care must be taken to cover the canvas completely.

USES: Background, object filling, border, outline, shading.

FIGURE 22a. Upright Gobelin stitch

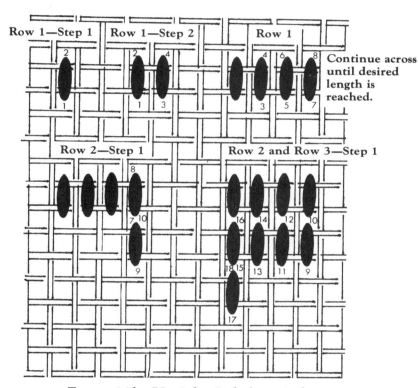

FIGURE 22b. Upright Gobelin stitch

INTERLOCKING GOBELIN STITCH
(ENCROACHING GOBELIN STITCH)
(Figures 23a and b)

Two strands on 10 mesh
One strand on 12 mesh

FAMILY: Gobelin.
COVERAGE: Two yards covers one square inch.
NOTES: All types of canvas may be used.
    Covers the back well.
    Pulls the canvas out of shape.
    Can be enlarged.
USES: Background, object filling, border, shading.

FIGURE 23a. **Interlocking Gobelin stitch**

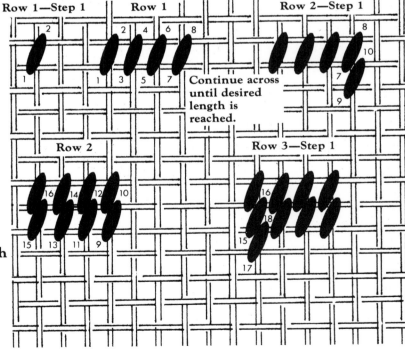

FIGURE 23b. **Interlocking Gobelin stitch**

FISHBONE STITCH *(Figures 24a and b)*

Three strands on 10 mesh
Two strands on 12 mesh

FAMILY: Oblique.

COVERAGE: Two and one-half yards covers one square inch.

NOTES: All types of canvas may be used.

Covers the back well.

Can be enlarged.

USES: Background, object filling.

FIGURE 24a. Fishbone stitch

FIGURE 24b. Fishbone stitch

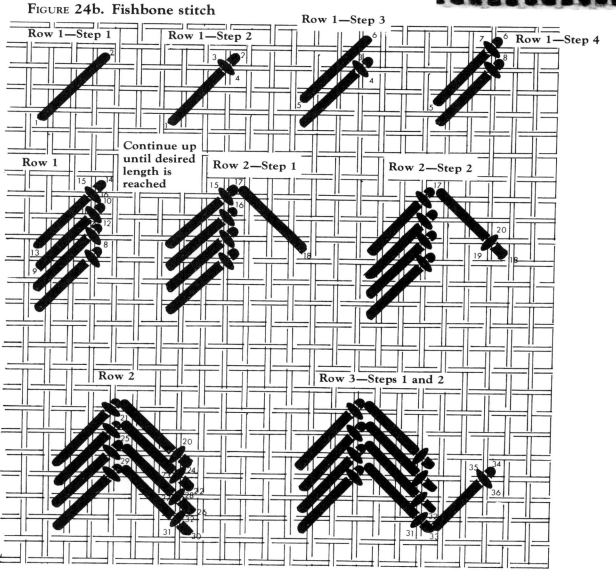

STEM STITCH *(Figures 25a and b)*

Three strands on 10 mesh
Two strands on 12 mesh

FAMILY: Oblique.
COVERAGE: Two yards covers one square inch.
NOTES: All types of canvas may be used.
    Can be enlarged.
    Can be done in two colors.
    Covers the back.
USES: Background, object filling, border.

FIGURE 25a. Stem stitch

FIGURE 25b. Stem stitch

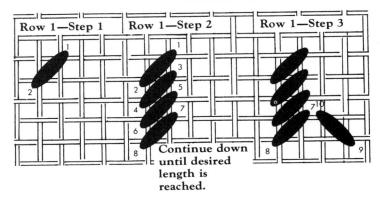

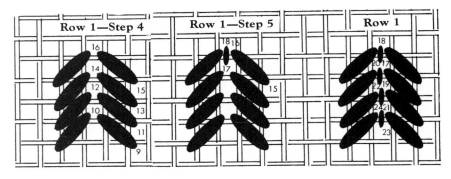

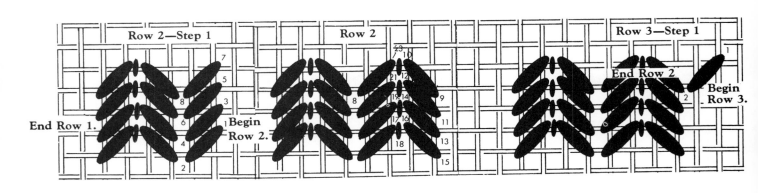

HERRINGBONE STITCH *(Figures 26a and b)*

Two strands on 10 mesh
One strand on 12 mesh

FAMILY: Herringbone.

COVERAGE: Four and one-half yards covers one square inch.

NOTES: This size best worked on penelope or interlock; enlarge to work on mono.

Can be enlarged.

Work from the top down.

Each row must be started anew.

USES: Background, object filling, border.

FIGURE **26a.** Herringbone stitch

FIGURE **26b.** Herringbone stitch

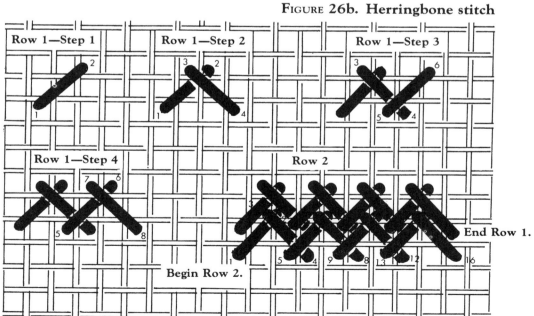

HERRINGBONE GONE WRONG STITCH
(Figures 27a and b)

Two strands on 10 mesh
One strand on 12 mesh

FAMILY: Herringbone.

COVERAGE: Four yards covers one square inch.

NOTES: This size best worked on penelope or interlock; enlarge to work on mono.

Can be enlarged.

Care must be taken to cover the canvas completely.

Work from top to bottom.

USES: Background, object filling, border.

FIGURE 27a. **Herringbone gone wrong stitch**

FIGURE 27b. **Herringbone gone wrong stitch**

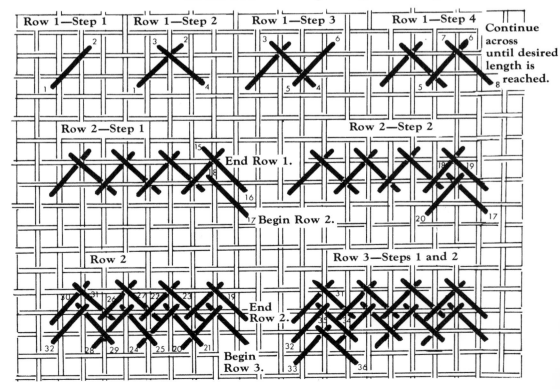

BRICK STITCH *(Figures 28a and b)*

Three strands on 10 mesh
Two strands on 12 mesh

FAMILY: Brick.

COVERAGE: Three yards covers one square inch.

NOTES: All types of canvas may be used.

Can be enlarged.

Care must be taken to cover the canvas completely.

USES: Background, object filling, border, shading.

LEFT HAND: Turn canvas upside down for second row.

FIGURE **28a. Brick stitch**

FIGURE **28b. Brick stitch**

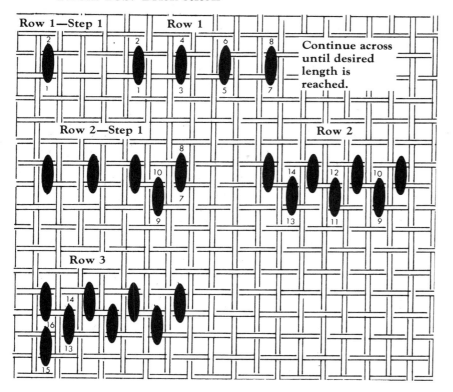

PARISIAN EMBROIDERY STITCH *(Figures 29a and b)*

Three strands on 10 mesh
Two strands on 12 mesh

FAMILY: Brick.
COVERAGE: Two and one-half yards covers one square inch.
NOTES: All types of canvas may be used.
　　　Make sure the canvas is completely covered.
　　　Can be enlarged or reduced.
USES: Background, object filling, border.
LEFT HAND: Turn canvas upside down for second row.

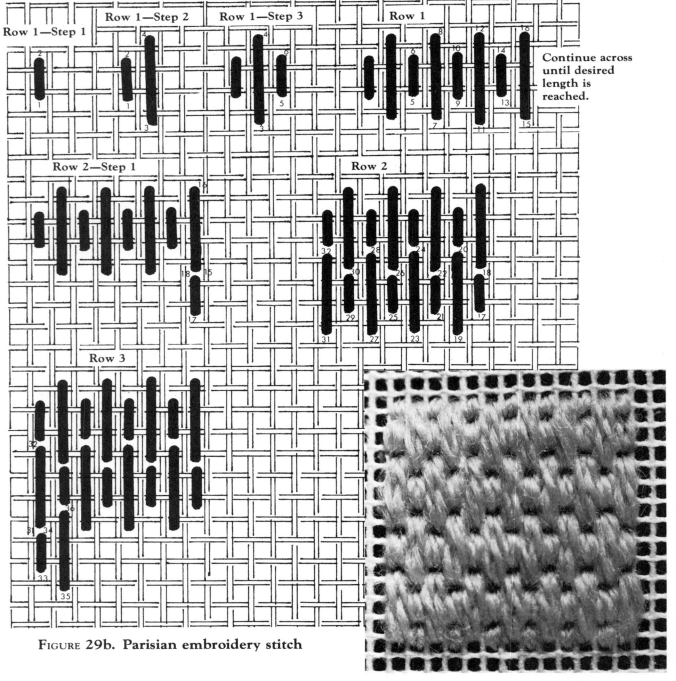

FIGURE 29b. Parisian embroidery stitch

FIGURE 29a. Parisian embroidery stitch

HUNGARIAN STITCH *(Figures 30a and b)*

Three strands on 10 mesh
Two strands on 12 mesh

FAMILY: Bargello.
COVERAGE: Three yards covers one square inch.
NOTES: All types of canvas may be used.
  Make sure the canvas is completely covered.
  Can be enlarged.
  Many colors can be used.
USES: Background, object filling, border.
LEFT HAND: Turn canvas upside down for second row.

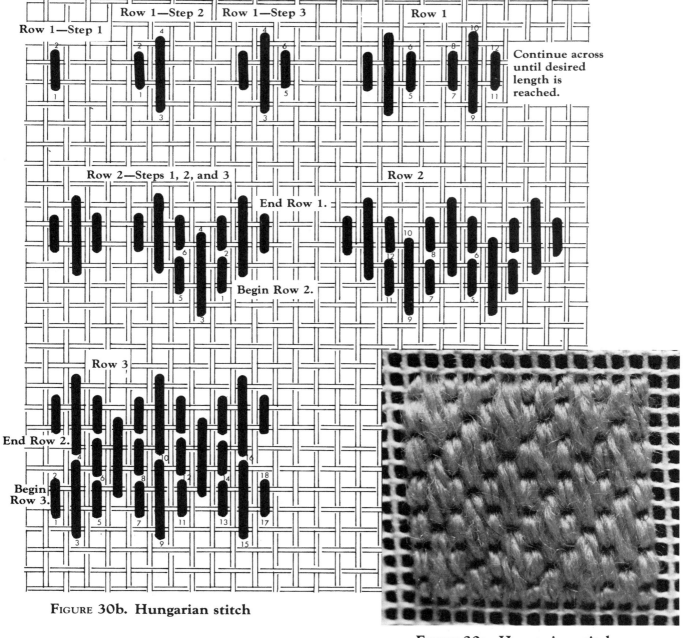

FIGURE 30b. Hungarian stitch

FIGURE 30a. Hungarian stitch

BYZANTINE STITCH *(Figures 31a and b)*

Three strands on 10 mesh
Two strands on 12 mesh

FAMILY: Bargello.
COVERAGE: Three yards covers one square inch.
NOTES: All types of canvas may be used.
    Can be enlarged or reduced.
    Make sure the stitches all slant in the same direction.
    Many colors can be used.
USES: Background, object filling, border.
LEFT HAND: Turn canvas upside down for second row.

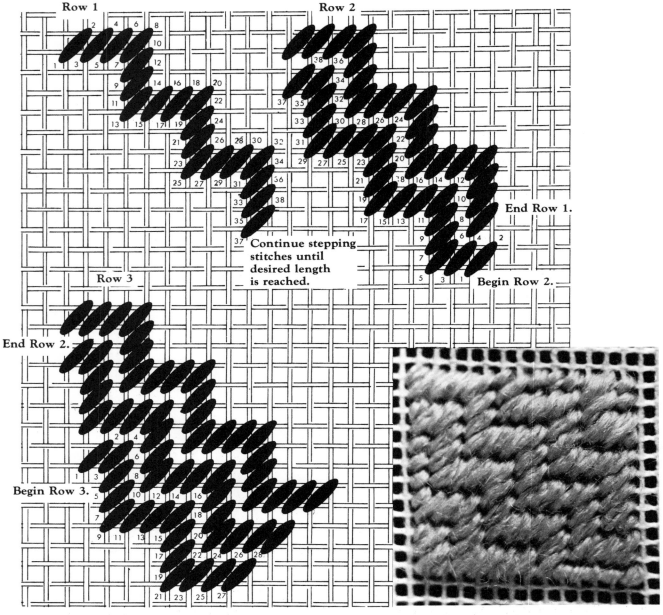

FIGURE 31b. Byzantine stitch   FIGURE 31a. Byzantine stitch

FLORENTINE STITCH (FLAME STITCH)
(Figures 32a and b)

Three strands on 10 mesh
Two strands on 12 mesh

FAMILY: Bargello.
COVERAGE: Two and one-half yards covers
    one square inch.
NOTES: All types of canvas can be used.
    Can be enlarged or reduced.
    Many colors can be used.
USES: Background, object filling, border.

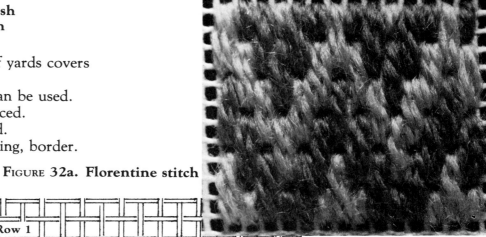

FIGURE **32a. Florentine stitch**

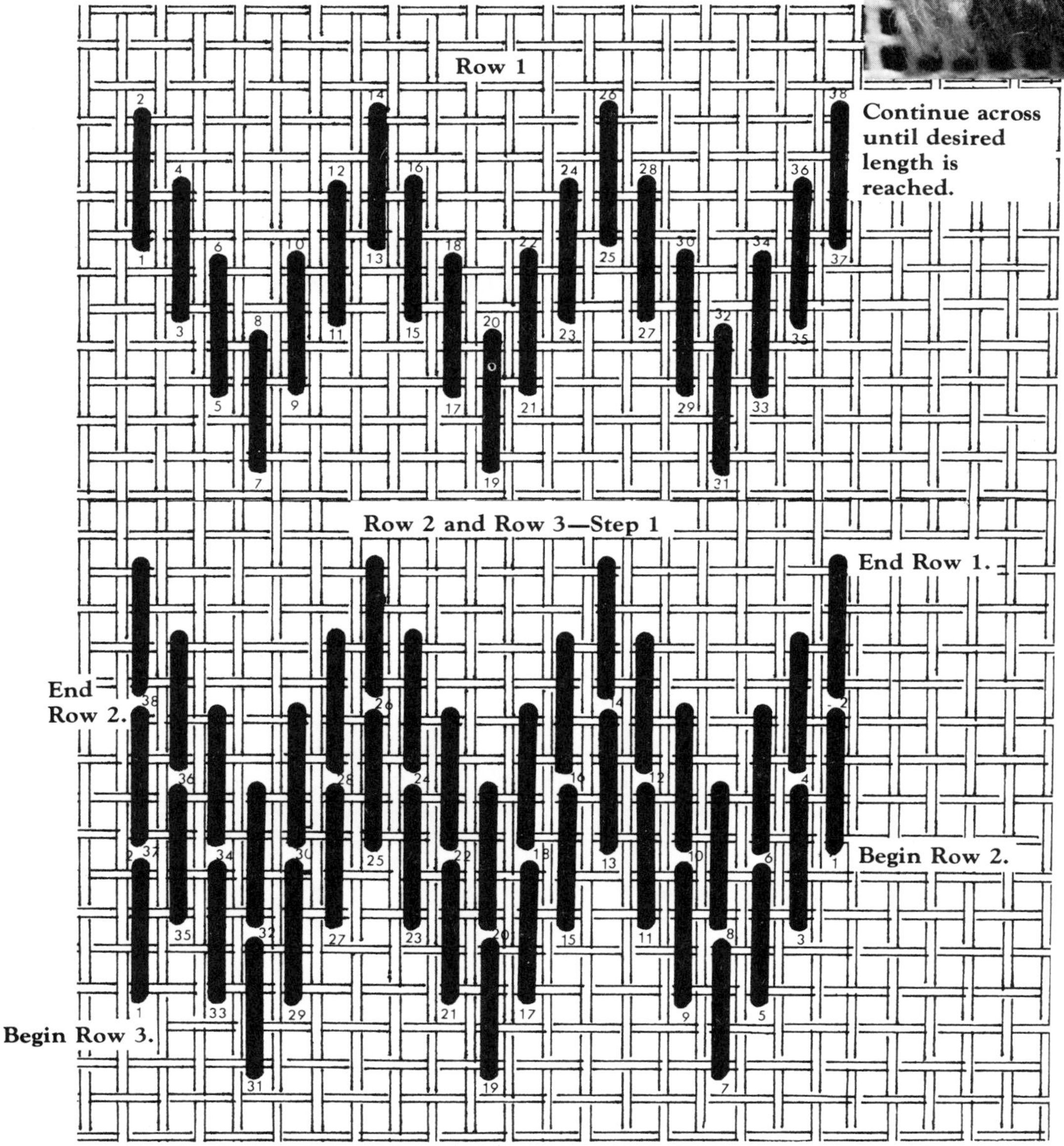

Row 1

Continue across
until desired
length is
reached.

Row 2 and Row 3—Step 1

End Row 1.

End
Row 2.

Begin Row 2.

Begin Row 3.

FIGURE **32b. Florentine stitch**

STAR STITCH (*Figures 33a and b*)

Two strands on 10 mesh
One strand on 12 mesh

FAMILY: Star.
COVERAGE: Two and two-thirds yards covers one square inch.
NOTES: Best worked on penelope and interlock; enlarge to work on mono.
   Care must be taken to cover the canvas completely.
   Can be enlarged.
   Always work in toward center of stitch.
USES: Background, object filling, border, isolated stitch.

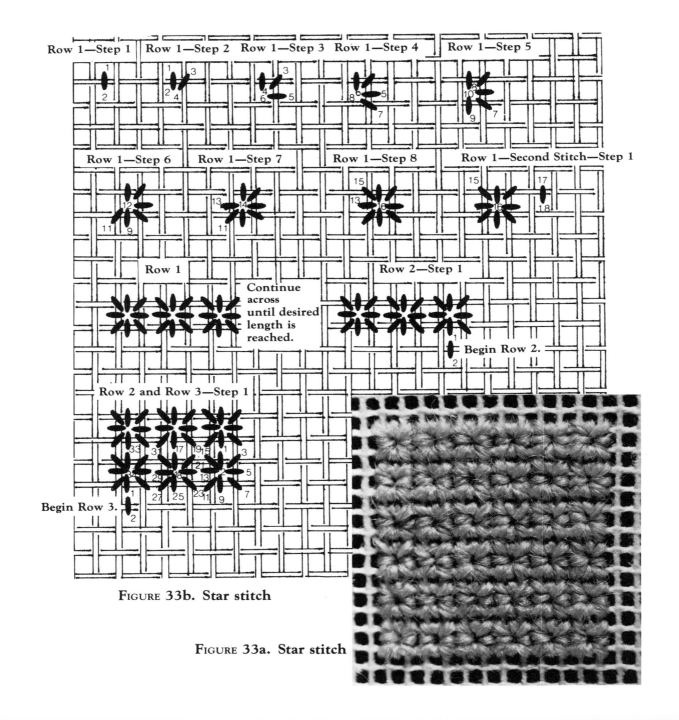

FIGURE 33b. Star stitch

FIGURE 33a. Star stitch

BOKHARA COUCHING STITCH *(Figures 34a and b)*

Three strands on 10 mesh
Two strands on 12 mesh

FAMILY: Couching.

COVERAGE: Two yards covers one square inch.

NOTES: All types of canvas may be used.

Couching stitches may be varied in placement.

Care must be taken to cover the canvas completely.

Two colors may be used.

USES: Background, object filling, border.

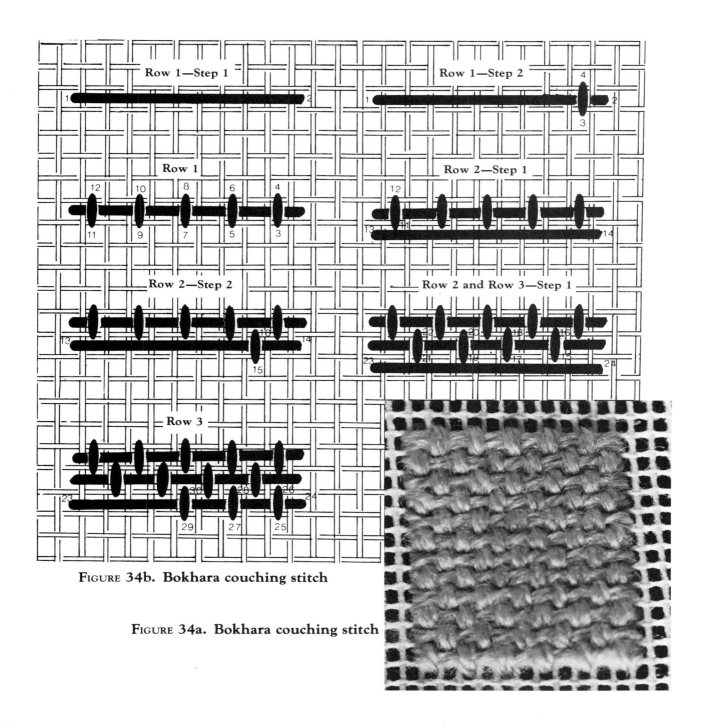

FIGURE **34b. Bokhara couching stitch**

FIGURE **34a. Bokhara couching stitch**

KNOTTED STITCH *(Figures 35a and b)*

Two strands on 10 mesh
One strand on 12 mesh

FAMILY: Couching.
COVERAGE: One and one-half yards covers one square inch.
NOTES: All types of canvas may be used.
    All stitches must slant in the same direction.
    Each stitch must be done individually.
    Can be enlarged.
    Care must be taken to cover the canvas completely.
USES: Background, object filling, border.
LEFT HAND: Turn canvas upside down for second row.

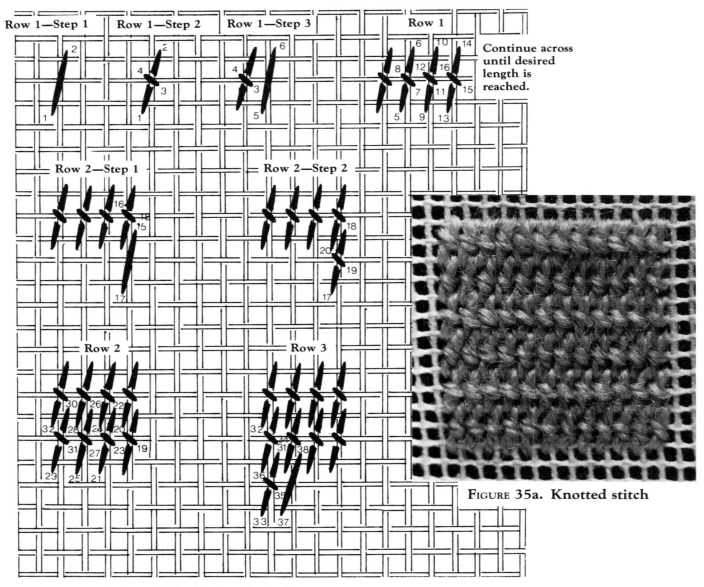

FIGURE 35a. Knotted stitch

FIGURE 35b. Knotted stitch

TURKEY WORK STITCH *(Figures 36a and b)*

Three strands on 10 mesh
Two strands on 12 mesh

FAMILY: Loop.

COVERAGE: Six yards covers one square inch.

NOTES: All types of canvas may be used.

Work from the bottom up.

Start each row anew.

Work from left to right.

Keep the loops even.

Can be cut or loops can be left.

USES: Background, object filling, border.

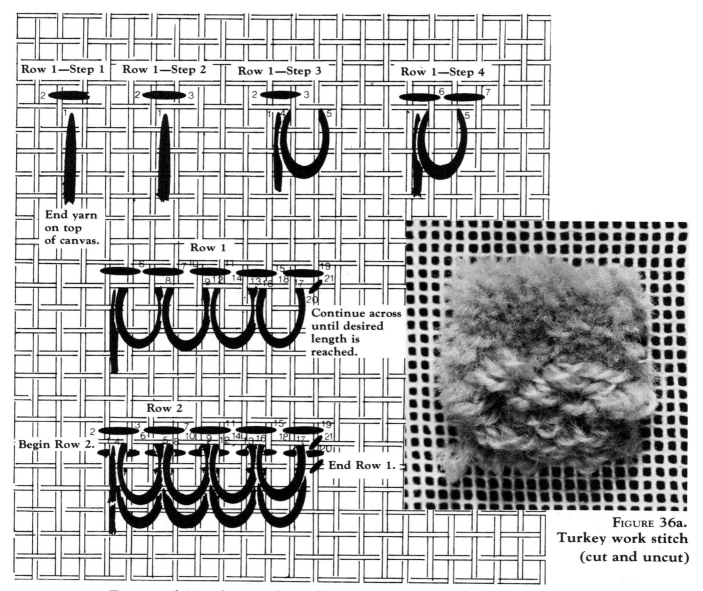

Row 1—Step 1   Row 1—Step 2   Row 1—Step 3   Row 1—Step 4

End yarn on top of canvas.

Row 1

Continue across until desired length is reached.

Row 2

Begin Row 2.

End Row 1.

FIGURE 36a.
**Turkey work stitch
(cut and uncut)**

FIGURE 36b. **Turkey work stitch**

SURREY STITCH *(Figures 37a and b)*

Two strands on 10 mesh
One strand on 12 mesh

FAMILY: Loop.
COVERAGE: Five yards covers one square inch.
NOTES: Use only penelope or interlock canvas.
    Work from the bottom up.
    Start each row anew.
    Work from left to right.
    Keep the loops even.
    Can be cut or loops can be left.
    Can be worked in smaller areas than turkey work stitch.
USES: Background, object filling, border, shading.

FIGURE 37a. **Surrey stitch (cut and uncut)**

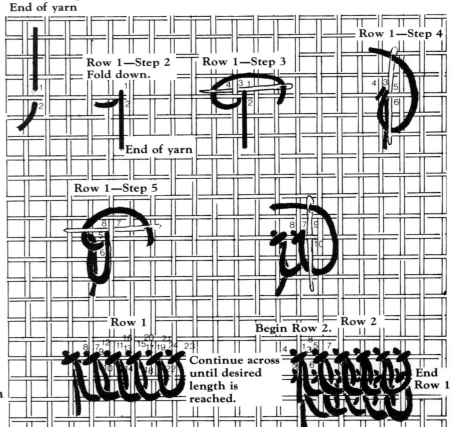

FIGURE 37b. **Surrey stitch**

Most stitches can be enlarged or reduced in size, as indicated in the note accompanying the stitch. For example, the cross stitch is shown over one thread but can be executed over two threads or more. When enlarging a stitch, it must be enlarged both horizontally and vertically. The same holds true for reducing a stitch. Care must also be taken to adjust the number of strands of yarn used to ensure complete coverage of the canvas. My preference is usually to use a stitch in its smallest version, as it seems more defined in this form (Figure 38).

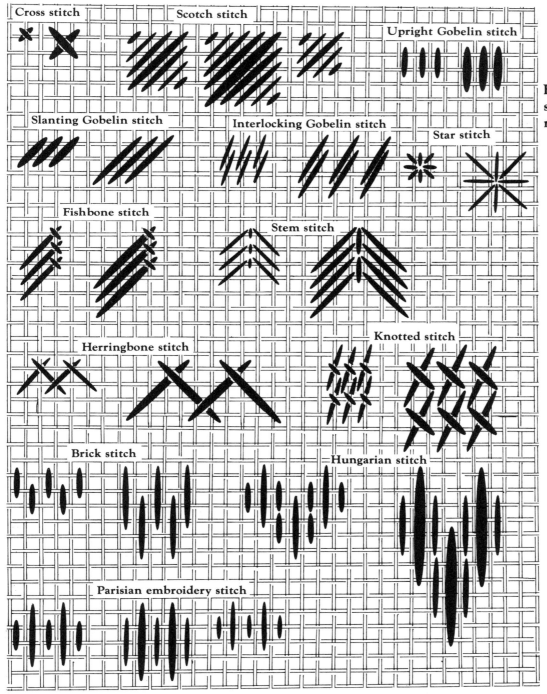

FIGURE 38. **Various stitches enlarged or reduced**

Many stitches can be raised up or padded by a procedure known as tramé. Tramé can also be employed to achieve better coverage with certain stitches such as the upright Gobelin. Tramé is a series of long horizontal threads laid on the canvas in the shape of the design. The long areas are usually laid unevenly. The colors used indicate the stitch color (Figure 39). The tramé thread is laid across the canvas (usually a maximum of six threads), and stitches are then done on top of this thread. On a painted canvas, lay on the tramé threads one at a time and stitch over them. The tramé procedure is European in origin. During the 1920s and 1930s most American canvaswork designs were sold traméd.

The size of the canvas mesh used can greatly affect both the design and the stitches (Figure 40). The finer the mesh, the more gently will curves fall in. Also, more details may be added on finer meshes. Very fine meshes, however, result in a loss of the stitches' construction; therefore, stitches on extremely fine mesh must be carefully chosen. I have found that canvas mesh in sizes 12, 14, 16, and 18 seems to satisfy most general canvas embroidery needs.

FIGURE 39. **Tramé threads laid on a painted canvas**

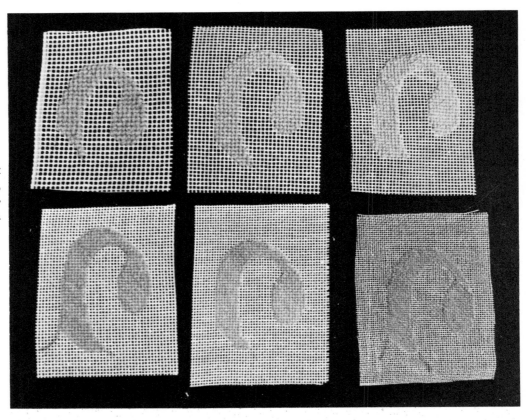

FIGURE 40. **Design unit stitched on size 10, 12, 14, 16, 18, and 24 mesh**

Fitting stitches into shapes at the outer limits of a design object is called compensation. If we look at objects in nature, we see that the texture or pattern does not change when it gets to its edge. Stitching, therefore, should not change as it approaches the edge of a design object. When starting to stitch an object, first decide where to begin. The center of an object is always a good choice. If you start in the center and work out, the stitches will naturally find the edge. When an edge is reached, very often a full-stitch construction cannot be used

(Figure 41). Rather than change the stitch, continue the stitch, doing only the portion needed. In short, if you were to continue the part of the stitch you have used, you would have a full stitch. Sometimes, to give a more rounded effect, we reduce the stitch in size as it approaches the edge as well as doing only portions of it. The photo of the Rhodes stitch in a circle shows how size change and proportioning are combined (Figure 42).

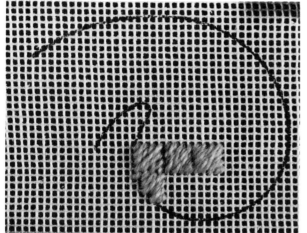

FIGURE 41. **Compensating Scotch stitches in a curve**

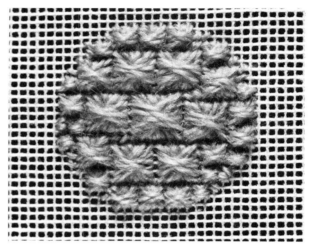

FIGURE 42. **Rhodes stitch compensated by reduction**

As with the art of drawing, changes or mistakes can occur in canvas embroidery; in this case we "erase" by ripping stitches out. Never just take your scissors to the canvas. Ripping takes more time than stitching, but if done carefully it can save the grief of a cut into the canvas.

There are two methods of ripping. The first is to unstitch. Using your needle unthreaded, lift and pull out each stitch in the order it was stitched, but starting from the last stitch and working to the first. For the second method, run a tapestry needle under several worked stitches, lifting up from the canvas, and snip the yarn, using very fine curved manicure scissors. Then use tweezers on the wrong side to pull the yarn out.

Should the canvas mesh be cut, it can be repaired by unweaving some canvas threads from the selvedge and reweaving them into the cut area. Be careful to duplicate the over and under of the canvas weave. Use this method of canvas repair rather than attach a new piece of canvas; it will result in a stronger repair with no puckering or bumps showing (Figure 43).

FIGURE 43. **Repairing canvas by reweaving**

When large areas are being worked in a particular stitch, it is sometimes more practical to work the stitch on the diagonal (Figure 44). While it does not work for all stitches, many can be done diagonally. This method of stitching also provides better coverage and usually keeps the canvas from pulling out of shape. Even when working on the diagonal, remember to work into stitches already completed, catching a bit of the fiber.

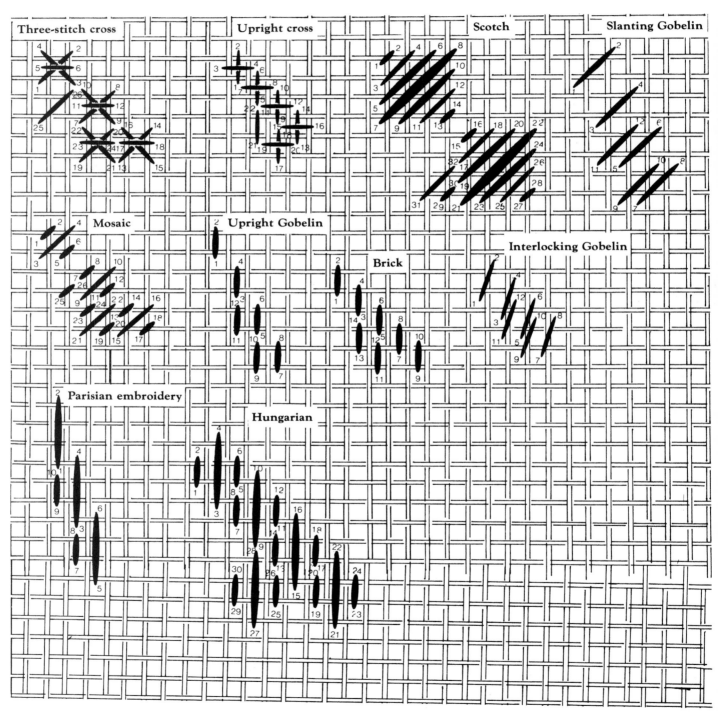

FIGURE **44. Stitches done diagonally**

EXERCISES

1. Practice each stitch in at least one-inch squares like those shown in the charts on size 10 mesh interlock canvas, 12 mesh penelope, and 14 mono-canvas using Persian yarn or crewel yarn to achieve coverage.

2. Practice enlarging and reducing one stitch from each of the following families: cross, Scotch, Gobelin, brick, oblique, herringbone, bargello, star, couching, or loop. Do one-inch-square samples on size 12 mesh using Persian yarn or crewel to achieve coverage. Record the amount of yarn required and the number of strands for each.

3. Practice tramé on one stitch from each of the following families: half cross, cross, continental, Scotch, Gobelin, brick, oblique, herringbone, bargello, loop. Do one-inch-square samples on size 14 mesh using Persian yarn or crewel yarn to achieve coverage.

4. Using a quarter as a size indicator, practice circles of continental stitch on size 10, 12, 14, 16, 18, 24 canvas meshes using Persian yarn or crewel yarns to achieve coverage.

5. Compare the effects of one stitch from each of the following families using size 10 and size 18 mesh canvases: half cross, cross, continental, Scotch, Gobelin, brick, oblique, herringbone, bargello, star, couching, loop, miscellaneous. Do four rows of each using Persian yarn or crewel yarns to achieve coverage.

6. Using a simple shape such as a circle or a free-form curved shape, compensate one stitch from each of the following families: half cross, cross, continental, Scotch, Gobelin, brick, oblique, herringbone, bargello, star, couching, loop, miscellaneous. Do each shape on size 12 mesh using Persian or crewel yarns to achieve coverage. Do two samples of each, one using the stitch as charted, the other reducing the stitch as the outer limits are reached.

7. Stitch on the diagonal one stitch from each of the following families: cross, continental, Scotch, Gobelin, brick, oblique, bargello, star, couching, loop, miscellaneous. Use size 16 mesh and Persian or crewel yarn to achieve coverage. Do four rows of each stitch.

Design

Design is a very personal concept; it is your interpretation of your ideas. A design professor of mine once had the perfect answer to those who say, "I'm no artist, I can't even draw a straight line." He replied, "Artists don't draw straight lines—they use rulers." When we bring design down from its lofty perch and take a practical look at the elements involved, step by step, it becomes another form of communication with its own vocabulary. You are simply speaking but using visual means in place of words. Doing your own designs for canvas embroidery allows you to speak completely for yourself.

To begin our investigation into this new vocabulary, we start with the basic elements of design. All objects fall into the following basic shapes: square, rectangle, triangle, and circle. To add dimension to these shapes we arrive at cubes, cones, cylinders, and so on (Figure 45). Look around you. Everything falls into these shapes.

FIGURE 45. **Basic shapes and basic shapes in dimension**

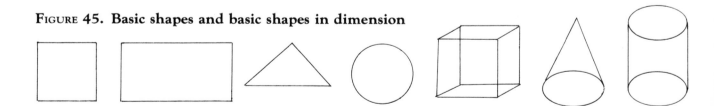

In using words, we convey meaning where we place them; so with design, where we place our shapes communicates feelings.

When placed in the center of a page, a shape becomes quiet and motionless. Lowered on the page, a shape projects a sense of falling. Higher, it seems to rise. As we approach the edge or fall off the edge of our design area, the shape becomes more conspicuous (Figure 46).

Size is also a communicator of feelings. Large shapes come forward, while smaller ones seem to float away (Figure 47).

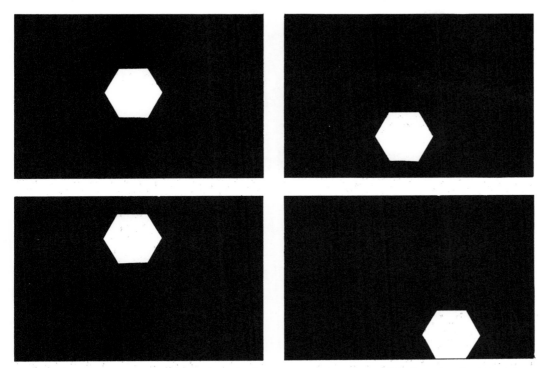

FIGURE 46. **Centered—quiet and unmoving; lowered—falling; higher—rising; on the edge— more conspicuous**

FIGURE 47.

Combinations of sizes and shapes cause interest and start to tell our story. Nature is the best leader. Look at the shape combinations out your window. Try changing nature to basic plane figures following the same shapes and positions you see (Figures 48a and b).

How shapes are placed in relation to each other can communicate our feelings. Shapes far apart make the background seem important. All too often, especially in embroidery, we tend to forget how very important the background is. How background is treated is tremendously important to any piece you do; it is an integral part of your design.

FIGURE 48a. Vegetation

FIGURE 48b. Vegetation in basic shapes

When shapes approach each other, a feeling of unity is imparted. Touching shapes produce tension, and overlapping shapes create the illusion of more than one level or plane (Figure 49).

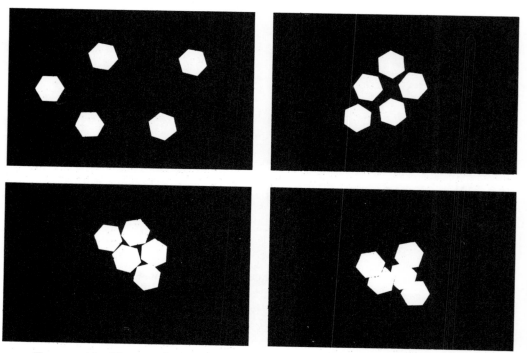

FIGURE 49. Shapes far apart—background most important; shapes close together—unity; shapes touching—tension; shapes overlapping—more than one level

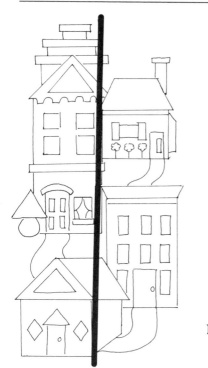

FIGURE 50c. **Circular eye direction**

FIGURE 50b. **Curved eye direction**

FIGURE 50a. **Straight eye direction**

When observing a design, we also find that our eyes follow certain directions: straight, curved, or circular (Figure 50). You will notice that when your eyes follow curves, you have a greater feeling of movement. This is also true of the lines we use. Curving causes speed, and the deeper the curves, the more it slows down (Figure 51).

FIGURE 51. **Top curves show faster movement than bottom curve.**

Balance is another element of design that is extremely important. Let's consider a seesaw (Figures 52a–c). Placing objects in an unbalanced manner will not work; the seesaw will not stay straight. Of course, we could always balance it the safest way possible, but we all know that it works that way. So let's try to balance the seesaw a new way. Our newly balanced seesaw is more interesting than the previous one.

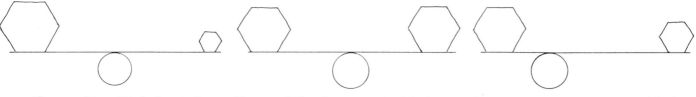

FIGURE 52a. **Unbalanced**   FIGURE 52b. **Symmetrical balance**   FIGURE 52c. **Asymmetrical balance**

The last element to think about is simplicity. Don't try to put everything into one design. Your eye will be happier with fewer shapes than with a great many objects all jumbled up.

Design can fall into two different categories: traditional or abstract. Let's deal first with traditional design with realistic, recognizable forms.

1. Choose a theme (e.g., the four seasons).
2. List all the objects that go with that theme (spring: daffodils, pussy-willows, tulips, crocus; summer: sunflowers, zinnias, marigolds; fall: mums, oak leaves, cattails, acorns; winter: holly, pine cones, pine needles).
3. Decide which objects on the list to choose for your design (pine cones, pine needles, pussywillows, sunflowers, cattails).
4. Turn the objects into basic shapes.
5. Decide where the emphasis and feeling should be by the direction the eye will follow.
6. Start placing the basic shapes until you have a satisfactory arrangement (Figure 53).

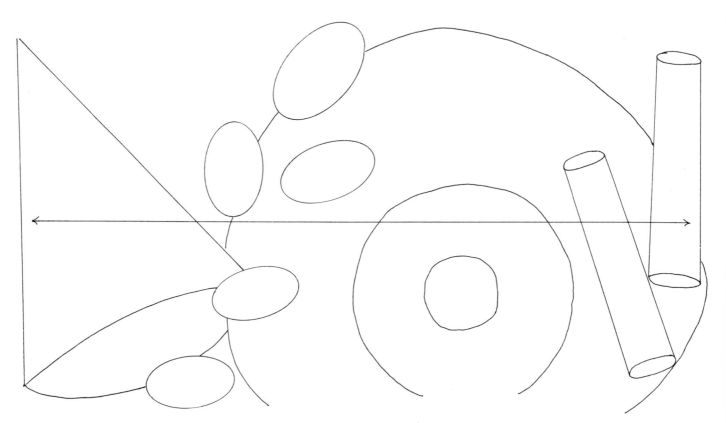

FIGURE 53. **Arrangement of basic shapes in a straight eye direction**

7. Turn the basic shapes in the arrangement into the traditional objects they represent. Collect photos or drawings of the objects as a reference (Figure 54).

FIGURE 54. "Four Seasons," stitched design by the author

Now let us turn to abstract designs. This is more flexible than traditional work even by definition. Two definitions of abstract art are: (1) the use of shape, color, line, and texture to obtain a composition that does not refer to a particular recognizable object, and (2) the simplification of recognizable forms to produce a composition.

One tool to use when working with both abstract and traditional designs is a viewfinder. Cut a shape out of white paper—a square or rectangle is the most useful, but a circle, oval, triangle, or free form can also be used. This hole is the shape that your canvas embroidery will be. Now, using magazine or book photographs, use your viewfinder to find a design. When you see something pleasing through your paper viewfinder, lay a piece of tracing paper on top and trace the design you have found (Figure 55).

   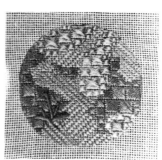

FIGURE 55. Use of a viewfinder to develop a design

Another method is to take colored papers (tissue paper works well) or newspaper and rip, cut, or tear until you have a pleasing design (Figure 56).

FIGURE 56. Use of
ripped paper to
develop a design

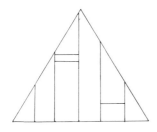

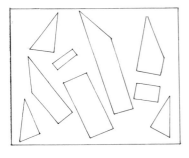

There are many more methods of coming up with designs; you should
experiment and try out many types of designing. For example, you might take a
basic shape, cut it apart, and "explode" it (Figures 57a and b).

FIGURE 57a. Triangle is
cut apart and exploded
shapes are arranged
into a design.

FIGURE 57b. Exploded
triangle design stitched
and mounted as a
pillow

When you have decided on a design, the next problem to be tackled is enlarging it to the size desired. The steps for this procedure are as follows.

1. Measure the size of your design (e.g., 2 inches by 3 inches).
2. Decide the final size of your canvas embroidery (say, 8 inches by 12 inches).
3. Use this formula to determine the proportions you must use:

$$\frac{\text{width of design}}{\text{length of design}} = \frac{\text{width of final design}}{\text{length of final design}}$$

$$\frac{2}{3} = \frac{8}{12}$$

4. Make a rectangle on drawing paper the finished size.
5. Now fold the design in four lengthwise and four widthwise folds.
6. Now fold the rectangle on the drawing paper the same way as in Step 5.
7. Draw the design up from the small to the large version square by square.
8. Cut away the excess margins of the paper so that the large design is the exact size it will be when finished (Figure 58).

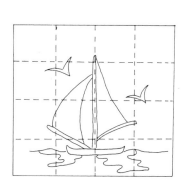
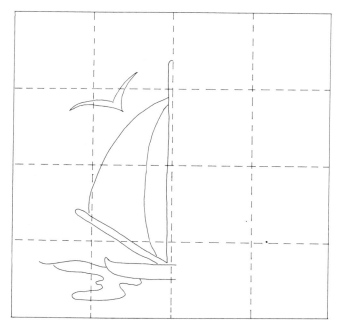

FIGURE 58. Steps for enlarging a design: (*above*) lengthwise and crosswise folds; (*right*) design being enlarged

FIGURE 59. Put a design where it will "live," before stitching.

At this point, put your design where the completed work is going to be. If it is to be hung on a wall, hang the drawing up on the wall and see how it functions within the edges of the paper it is on. The edges of a design are as important as what is contained within. By staring at it you will be able to see what marks, lines, or elements are not working. This is the time to change what needs changing. I cannot stress too strongly the value of putting the design where it will "live" and making the necessary changes. A design for a pillow top, for instance, should be placed on a chair and viewed at the angle it will usually be seen (Figure 59).

Sources for our designs are as endless as our imagination and the world and even the universe around us (Figures 60 and 61). Collect photos, drawings, and natural objects such as shells to use for inspiration. As this collection of sources grows, so will your design possibilities.

FIGURE 60 (*left*). **Design source: bubbles on a cake of soap**

FIGURE 61 (*right*). **"Soap Bubbles," by the author**

I would like to add a word here about the mechanical aids that are available to the designer. The first is the photostating process. A design can be enlarged to the size needed by taking it to a photostater. If the design is a photograph or painting, have it printed light and then go over the lines with a black marker, leaving out the very fine details.

Another method is to use an opaque projector. This machine is rather expensive to buy, but many firms rent them. A drawing or photo is inserted in the machine and adjusted until the desired size is attained. Instead of projecting the image on a screen, project it onto a large sheet of paper and trace it.

EXERCISES

1. Using a black marking pen, outline basic shapes on photos in old magazines.
2. Looking out your window or at a plant, draw what you see in basic shapes, noticing how these shapes are combined and positioned.
3. Using a black marking pen, sketch eye directions—straight, circular, or curved—on photos in old magazines.
4. Using photos from old magazines, determine how balance is achieved: is it symmetrical, asymmetrical, or radial?
5. Do a design using one of the following themes: circus, summer, the sea, harvest, the city, happiness. Follow the procedure for traditional design given in this chapter.
6. Using viewfinders, do several designs—at least one traditional and one abstract.
7. Do a design using ripped colored papers.
8. Explode a circle, a triangle, and a rectangle to obtain a design.
9. Enlarge one of the designs you have done in the previous exercises.
10. Start a collection of design references. File these in folders labeled by subject.

Color

Everywhere we look there is color. In fact, nothing we see has any meaning without color. Our embroidery cannot function without color, but it seems that, until recently, the language of color usage—schemes, wheels, and so forth—has been incomprehensible to the embroiderer. Color, too, has been put on a lofty perch, but a short new vocabulary is all that is really needed.

The familiar color wheel (Figure 62a) was developed by Sir Isaac Newton in 1660 and became the basis for color usage. Today we know a great deal more

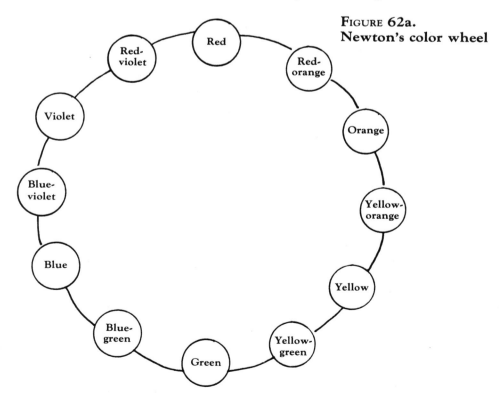

FIGURE 62a.
Newton's color wheel

about how the human eye sees and thus about how color works. It has always amazed me that embroiderers worked with the same color chart as a painter mixing paints would. A painter mixing yellow and blue paint on his or her palette will obtain green. The embroiderer or weaver combining yellow and blue threads will not; the embroiderer will achieve a gray effect from a distance. Clearly, in embroidery we need to begin a vocabulary of color from a new point of view.

In embroidery we are working with colors next to each other, in contrast to watercolor painting, where the paints are transparent and are seen through in layers. We must therefore regard color relationships on a partitive basis. This means that we view the ways colors look when placed next to other colors. Looking at the newly developed color wheel (Figure 62b) we find that the complementary colors are still opposite each other, but what those colors are is changed. This is important to us because complementary colors dull each other. Earlier it was pointed out that the painter mixing blue and yellow would achieve green. In partitive color, however, the complementary colors blue and yellow will yield a neutral. This is important when we want to tone down an effect or conversely want to brighten it up.

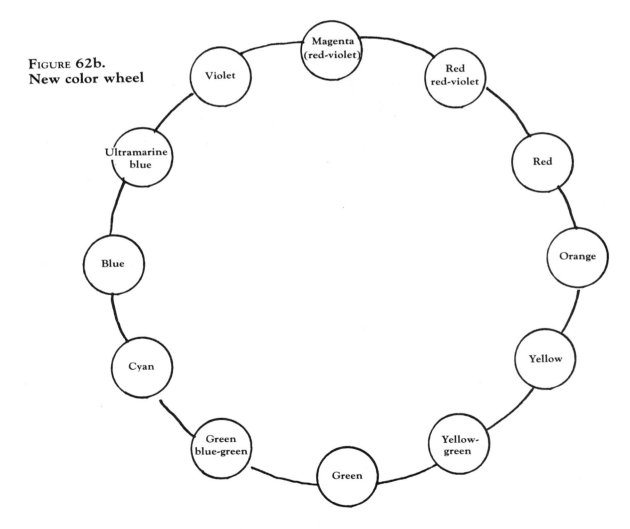

FIGURE 62b.
New color wheel

Color has three characteristics: hue, value or brightness, and intensity or saturation. Color does not work unless all three dimensions are working. Hue is the kind of color—red, yellow, magenta, green, and so on. To begin to use color in a piece of embroidery employing only hue spells disaster.

The next aspect of color is value or brightness. Very simply, how light or dark a color is determines its values. We change values by adding only white or black. When we cannot tell whether there is any white or black in a color, it is in its pure hue. But what can this value do for us? As we look around us we tend to see objects in "front" and "behind." This determining of position is the result of value, and we must determine the values of the hues in the parts of our design. For instance, if we were to make our background very light (white or almost white), the objects we wish to see in the foreground would be very dark. We would have the effect of looking through a dark forest out toward light. However, if the background were very dark, the foreground objects would be very light. The old masters employed this relationship in their still-life paintings. The most difficult situation for an embroiderer to deal with is the background that is neither light nor dark but middle value. Here the values put on the objects of the design must be very carefully placed to determine their positions. It takes a great deal of experience and experimentation to work with middle-value backgrounds (Figures 63a–c).

 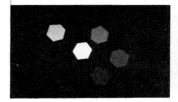 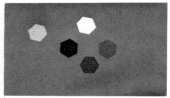

FIGURE 63a. Background white or light, dark values in foreground

FIGURE 63b. Background black or dark; light values in foreground

FIGURE 63c. Middle-value background.

The third quality of color is intensity or saturation. Here we find out how bright or dull a hue is—in other words, if there is any of the complement present. The greater the amount of the complement present in the color, the duller it is. The complement of any hue is the hue that is directly opposite it on the color wheel.

These three qualities of color at work produce some effects that can help us in our embroidery. Let us surround a small part of our design with a larger area of another hue. This smaller part will be influenced by the larger surrounding area. If we put yellow around a gray spot and blue around another gray spot, the gray in the yellow will seem darker (Figure 64). In short, a value surrounded by a lighter value will appear darker than the same value surrounded by a darker value.

Now let us surround one red spot with green and another red spot with a different value of red. Within the green, the red spot seems brighter. Within the red spot, not only will the red seem duller but it will take on a blue-green cast. How can this work for us? Well, if we want some area to have a very colorful accent, we can make it stronger by putting a contrast next to or around it. A contrasting hue is the hue that contains nothing of the original hue in it.

FIGURE 64. A value surrounded by a lighter value (*top*) appears darker than the same one surrounded by a darker value.

We used to hear that certain colors do not look well together. Well, they can when we employ a little more of our color knowledge. Experiment with the colors by changing one's value. Or maybe an easier way would be to place a small area or outline of a neutral (grays, black, or white) between the hues. Now these hues will probably not be disharmonious. In fact, when we isolate colors with neutrals, they tend to appear more colorful. A dull rose will appear more rose if it is surrounded by a gray outline or small area of gray. This enables us to employ yarn colors that we thought were dull and change their dullness. Also, if we wish to dull an area down, a complement or near complement employed in this manner works wonders.

We can also use value to lead the eye to focus its attention on certain areas. Our eyes will focus more quickly on warm colors such as reds, yellows, and oranges than on darker, cooler colors such as greens and blues.

When working in embroidery, it is very important to choose your yarn colors in the types of lighting they will be used in. Colors can and do change as the lighting changes. Try your yarns under all the light conditions in which they will appear. A living room pillow's yarn should be chosen under incandescent light and daylight, not fluorescent light. An evening handbag's yarn colors should be chosen in fluorescent and incandescent light, not daylight.

Texture—how rough or smooth—influences a color's reactions. The rougher the texture, the deeper or stronger a color will appear. Always experiment with a yarn in the texture or stitch it is going to be used in and see what happens to the hue. A pink, for instance, will seem paler in the encroaching Gobelin stitch and much pinker in the surrey stitch.

Where your embroidery "lives" will influence the hues used. For instance, a predominantly yellow embroidery will dull down in a blue room.

The greatest color teacher is nature. Turn to nature and study the color relationships in tree bark, for example, and try to duplicate these relationships in stitches and yarns. These exercises will help you to try colors in combinations and positions you never thought of before.

When you have decided on a design and the basic color relationships you wish to use, color your design, using crayons or markers, trying to match them to yarn colors. Then hang the design up or put it where it will be used and stare at it. You will be able to determine where your color relationships are going astray in this manner long before you actually begin stitching.

EXERCISES

1. Collect objects and write down the names of the hues you see. Look very carefully to determine whether, for example, red is red or is red, red-orange, etc.
2. Take a design and color it in values of black to white, making one background black, then one white, and finally mid-gray.
3. Stitch two-inch squares with one-inch squares in the center in at least twelve different hues in combinations—for example, a green square within a yellow square, a green within a violet. Try different values together as well.
4. Combine two disharmonious colors by adding neutrals or changing values until they are harmonious.
5. Combine a dull-hued yarn with neutrals until you get it to appear brighter.
6. Stitch one-inch squares using a warm red and a cool red, a warm yellow and a cool yellow.
7. Stitch a one-inch square of a pale hue in a rough texture and a smooth texture.
8. Take a natural object and match its colors to yarns, taking note of how they are positioned and the quantity and stitch in lines thick or thin, short or long, to duplicate these relationships.

Putting Designs on Canvas

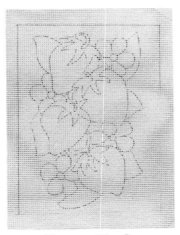

FIGURE 65. Canvas taped on top of design

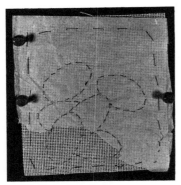

Figure 66. Tissue paper method

When you have a design drawn on paper, outline it in black using a black marker. Then tape the design down on your worktable firmly so it does not move. Lay the canvas down on top of the design and align the threads with the straight lines on the design. When the threads are all lined up, tape the canvas down on top of the design (Figure 65). When the canvas is a very fine mesh, it is difficult to see the design lines through the canvas. In this case it is better to use a light box. These are available in art supply stores, or you can use a slide-sorting tray available in photo supply stores. Taping the design to a sunny window also works well and is less expensive. The design is then outlined on the canvas following the threads of the canvas, using a gray Nepo marker or waterproof India ink and a crow-quill pen. Do not press heavily or bleeding will occur. I prefer to use the Nepo marker, but on fine-meshed canvas India ink is better. Make sure that any marking pen used on canvas is permanent and waterproof.

There are two additional ways to transfer outlines onto canvas. One is to use an iron-on transfer following the directions that come with it. Such transfers made specifically for use on canvas have recently come on the market. You can also make your own iron-ons using a transfer pencil—on the *reverse* side of the design. Make sure the directions accompanying these pencils are followed exactly.

Another method is to trace your design onto tissue paper, baste it onto the canvas, and then outline the design with running stitches and sewing thread (Figure 66). The tissue paper is then pulled away and the running stitches remain on the canvas. Care must be taken when pulling the tissue away. This method works best on very fine-meshed canvas.

You are now ready to stitch your design or paint in the colors. When painting or coloring a canvas, use the following steps for each object in the design, no matter what medium is used to color the canvas.

1. Find the darkest area and color it.
2. Find the lightest area and color it.
3. Fill in the middle areas.

68

This is the order for painting the strawberries design:

1. Darkest red on strawberries
2. Lightest red on strawberries
3. Medium red on strawberries
4. Black on strawberries
5. Darkest green on stems and leaves
6. Light green on leaves
7. Gray on flowers
8. Yellow centers on flowers
9. Blue-green background (Figure 67)

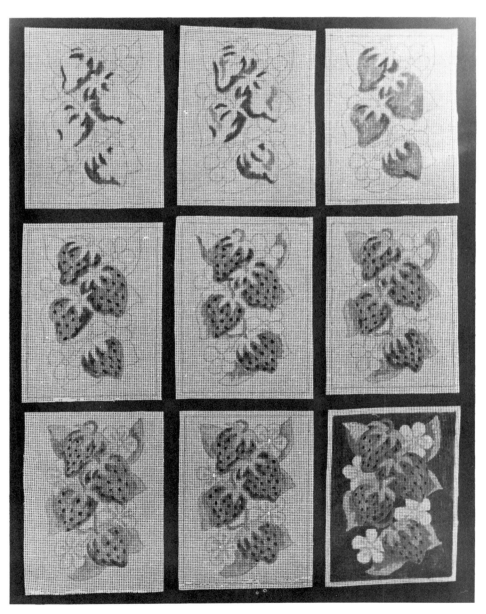

FIGURE 67. **Steps for painting a canvas design**

The media used to color are permanent felt-tip marking pens, acrylic paints, and oil paints. Felt-tip marking pens are not available in the tremendous range of colors and shades that paint mixing provides, but they do have quite a large variety. It is imperative that they be permanent, and even then care must be taken in using them. Use the broad tips and do not press too heavily or bleeding will occur. I have also found that navy, red, and magenta do not always hold permanently. When your design is colored in, spray it with a fixative (available in art supply stores). Work with marking pens and sprays in a well-ventilated area. Allow the canvas to dry at least twenty-four hours before stitching.

For my work, I prefer to use either acrylics or oils. When you use either of these, make sure the paint does not clog the canvas. Acrylics are used thinned with water to the consistency of heavy cream and are painted on with a nylon or bristle brush. Remember to wash out your brush with water when you finish painting or it will be ruined. Acrylics have the advantage of drying very quickly and provide vivid coloring on canvas. Allow the canvas to dry at least twenty-four hours.

Oil paints are a delight to work with, but their disadvantage is the length of drying time. I usually allow a week's time to dry. However, very fine shading can be painted on with oils (Figure 68).

FIGURE 68. **Design painted in marking pens, acrylics, and oil paint**

Large amounts of background can be painted in with a small damp sponge rather than a brush.

Because the edge of canvas is naturally very rough, finishing the edges is the next step. Your choices are to tape the edges with masking tape, zigzag-stitch the edges by machine, fold the edges under and sew, or encase the edges in seam binding (Figure 69). I have found that masking tape works best on interlock canvas; folding the edges under or using seam binding works best on mono-canvas. When using masking tape, I run my fingernail firmly down the edge to secure the fold.

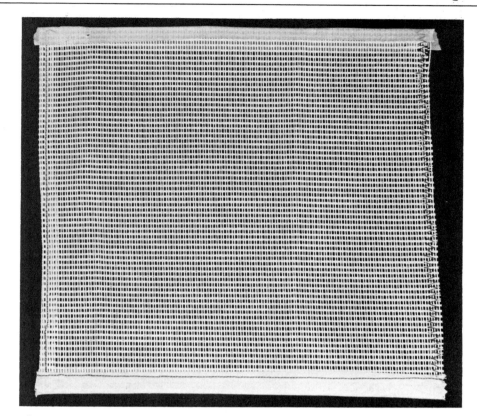

FIGURE 69. **Methods of edging a canvas.** *Top:* **masking tape,** *bottom:* **seam binding,** *left:* **hemming,** *right:* **zigzag machine stitching**

When you stitch a painted canvas, the color of yarn you use is determined by the color that is painted on each individual mesh of the canvas.

EXERCISES

1. Outline two designs on canvas, one on size 12 mesh using a marker and one on size 18 mesh using India ink.
2. Using either acrylics or oils, paint on canvas a design that requires shading.
3. Edge four designed canvases employing each of the following methods: masking tape on interlock, zigzag stitching on penelope, hemming on mono, and seam binding on mono.

Variations

When we speak, we have an enormous vocabulary of words to choose from that are largely the result of varying basic words. So it is with our canvas embroidery; our vocabulary is comprised of stitches that can be varied to provide us with a vast number of stitches. In fact, I have long felt that if the canvas embroiderer knew how to vary a stitch, he or she would only need to be taught the basic tent stitch.

We have four ways of varying a stitch: by size, by direction, by proportion, and by combination.

Let us take the basic tent stitch and see what happens to it with these four ways of varying. Basically it is as at the left; now let us change its direction, then let us combine these two; now change its proportion, and finally let us change its size (Figure 70).

FIGURE 70. **Basic tent stitch: changed by direction, changed by combination, changed by proportion, changed by size**

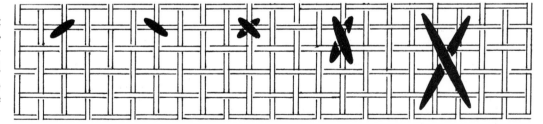

Investigation of the cross stitch will show us that our basic cross stitch can change its size, its direction, and its proportion, and can be combined (Figure 71). Now take each one of these variations and continue to vary these by combination, proportion, direction, size, and so forth.

FIGURE 71. **Cross stitch changed by size, direction, proportion, combination**

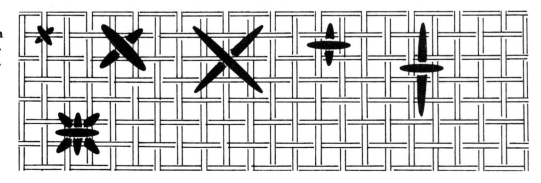

As you can see, the possibilities are great, as we have shown here with the cross stitch (Figure 72). These examples are the cross stitch varied within itself. It also can be combined with the other basic stitches such as Scotch, and be varied. Experiment with the stitches you have learned and see what happens (Figure 73).

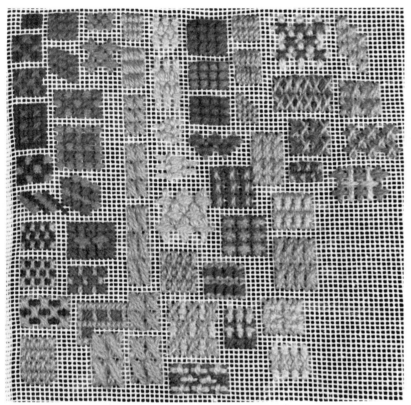

FIGURE 72. **Cross stitch variations**

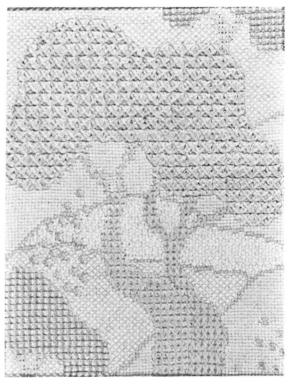

FIGURE 73. **"White Land," design using only variations of cross stitch, by the author**

EXERCISES

1. Choose one stitch from each of the stitch families (half cross, cross, continental, Scotch, Gobelin, brick, oblique, herringbone, bargello, star, couching, loop, and miscellaneous) and vary it by size, combination, proportion, and direction. Do these as one-inch squares on size 12 canvas and record the amount of yarn used and diagram the stitch on graph paper. (It is also a good idea to keep a continuing notebook of stitch variations for future reference.)
2. Stitch a design in variations of one stitch.

Texture

Designs come alive when texture is added. All designs are the result of form and shape. Texture, composed of yarn, color, and stitches, gives form.

The same stitch in different yarns can produce different effects. For instance, a rounded effect can be obtained by putting different fibers ranging from matte to shiny next to each other, using the same stitch. Try surrounding a small square of shiny silk or perle cotton in tent stitch with several rows of embroidery floss in the same color, then add several rows of linen again in the same color, now Persian yarn, tapestry wool, and finally matte cotton yarn all in the same color. As you can see, the flat square shape now has dimension. A word of caution about the use of different fibers. Don't get carried away and use too many different fibers for any one design. Use a minimum of different fibers for the best texture. Nature, again, is our best inspiration (Figure 74).

FIGURE 74. "Aerial View," design done in one stitch using cloisonné, wool, embroidery floss, and perle cotton, by the author

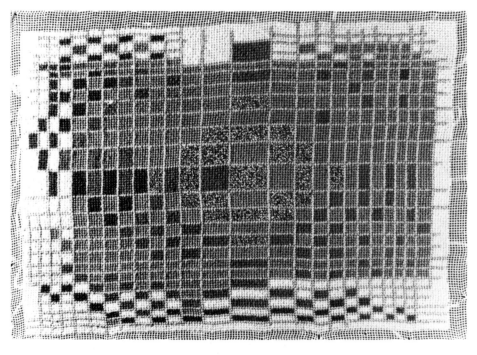

Stitches produce texture in a way no paintbrush can match. The manipulation of stitches is a very carefully thought-out procedure. Texture in canvaswork doesn't just happen; it is very carefully planned. Earlier we learned basic stitches; now let us relate these same stitches to texture. I put a number value on each stitch in a range from 1·(smoothest) to 6 (roughest). The stitches you learned previously have the following ratings:

1	2	3	4	5	6
Basketweave	Herringbone	Bokhara	Byzantine	Scotch	Surrey
Continental	Herringbone	Couching	Mosaic	Three-Stitch	Turkey
Half Cross	Gone	Brick	Mosaic	Cross	
Interlocking	Wrong	Cross Stitch	Diagonal		
Gobelin	Knotted	Fishbone	Upright		
	Star	Florentine	Cross		
	Upright	Hungarian			
	Gobelin	Parisian			
		Embroidery			
		Stem			

Try doing a strip of stitches in the following order of 1 to 6: interlocking Gobelin, knotted, brick, mosaic, Scotch, and surrey (Figure 75). You will notice that as the stitches change, the row seems to climb gradually.

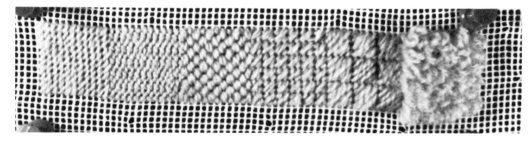

**FIGURE 75.
Ratings 1 to 6 stitched**

These ratings of stitches also tell us a great deal about the impact a stitch will have. Very smooth stitches (ratings 1 or 2) will not have the impact that a stitch with a high rating of 6 will impart. It follows then that stitches with high ratings should be used with great care, for the eye is pulled directly to them (Figure 76).

Changing the direction of a stitch will also provide texture. On a scrap piece of canvas try the following: small squares of continental facing in different directions but touching each other; the Parisian embroidery stitch done horizontally and vertically; the Scotch stitch changing direction (Figure 77). In Figure 78 we can see the definite changes in appearance between the directions. When changing direction, each stitch does not necessarily have to change; texture can be achieved by changing stitch directions in the areas.

The size of a stitch can also change the texture of a design. Large and small versions of the same stitch can produce shadows. Further shadows are achieved by combining stitches that are small, such as tent, with larger stitches, such as Scotch.

**FIGURE 76.
"Shacks," by the author**

FIGURE 77. **Changing stitch directions.** *Left to right:* Scotch, Parisian embroidery, continental

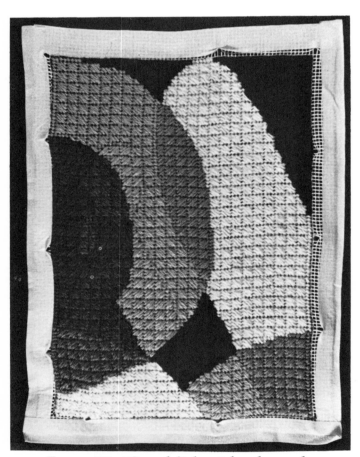

FIGURE 78. **"Searchlights," by the author**

FIGURE 79. **"Highways," by the author**

These shadows will produce form (Figure 79). The size of a stitch can also affect its texture rating. The larger the stitch, the greater the impact.

When learning stitches, we find that most stitch diagrams show the stitches placed in precise rows (Figure 80). Texture can be achieved when we take the same stitch but move it out of its precise order. When working in this manner, I find I am most comfortable drawing a line of movement on my

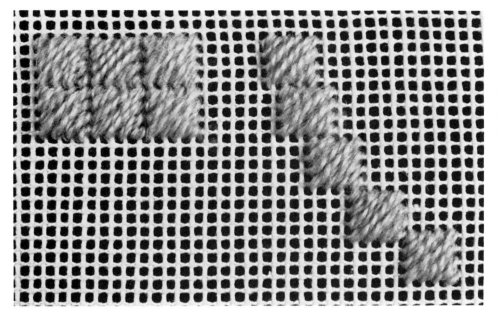

FIGURE 80. Scotch
stitch and Scotch stitch
moved

FIGURE 81. "Moving
Highways," by the
author

design and then juxtaposing the stitch to this line. In Figure 81 the stitches are
constructed exactly the same but are placed under each other in varying
positions.

All these methods of achieving texture can be combined with each other and with color to provide our embroideries with the texture they require and deserve. Be aware, however, that you don't have to use vast numbers of stitches in a single piece—use stitches to achieve definite effects, not just to show different stitches. As mentioned, nature is our greatest teacher. Note how textures are combined in the natural objects around you.

When I have completed a design, I mark it with the range number I want in each area to give it its impact. I then choose stitches that relate to the design to fill those rating numbers and actually sketch the stitch on the design. In this manner I am able to plan my texture effects before stitching (Figure 82).

FIGURE 82a.
"Camelot," by the author

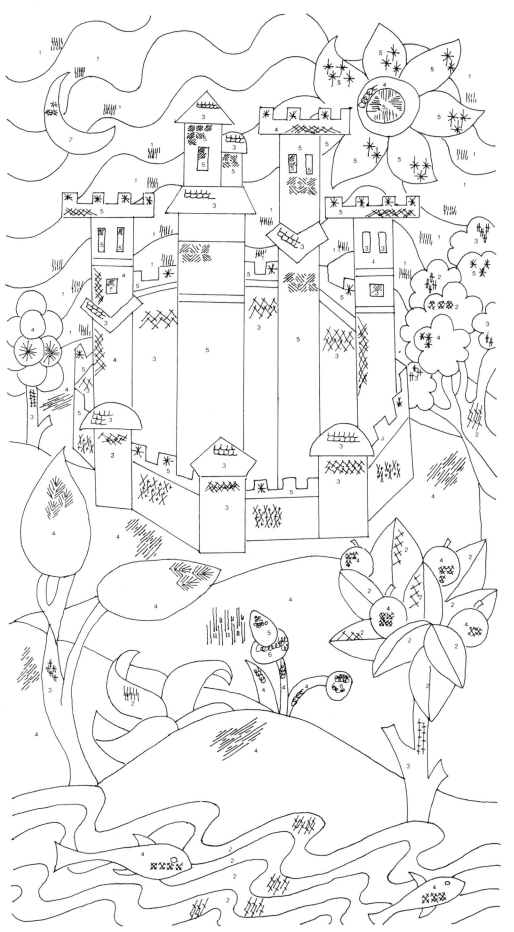

FIGURE 82b. Design
with rating numbers
and stitch placements

EXERCISES

1. Combine two fibers together in one-inch squares to see the effects obtained, e.g., matte cotton surrounded by a crewel wool. Do at least five different combinations.
2. Using one-inch squares touching each other, combine stitches of various ratings such as a 1 and a 2, a 1 and a 3, or a 1 and a 4, 5, or 6. Use various fibers as well to see how a rating can be intensified or subdued by the fiber used.
3. Using one stitch from each of the following families—half cross, cross, continental, Scotch, Gobelin, brick, oblique, herringbone, bargello, star, couching, and loop—do samples at least two inches square, changing the direction of the stitch to show texture change. Be aware that direction can change horizontally, vertically, or diagonally by areas or stitch by stitch.
4. Draw a curved line within a three-inch square on a piece of canvas and stitch the square, using the curved line as a guide to achieve movement. Do one sample for each of the following stitch families: cross, Scotch, star.
5. Sketch a natural design such as a flower, tree bark, a rock, or a leaf, and then study it and write down on your sketch such texture facts as *shiny, smooth, rough, color relationships, size, movement*.
6. Using the design developed in Exercise 5, turn your notes into fibers and stitches. Sketch stitches onto your design showing direction and movement lines where necessary. Put the design on canvas and stitch, using your notes.

Shading

Shading gives form to our designs; it adds realism to any form or shape we choose. We have three basic forms of shading: (1) simple (block or area) shading, (2) scatter shading, and (3) mixed and scattered shading.

Simple shading is just that—the simplest form of shading (Figure 83). It is used when a suggestion of realism is needed. Here are the steps to accomplish it:

FIGURE 83. **Simple (block) shading**

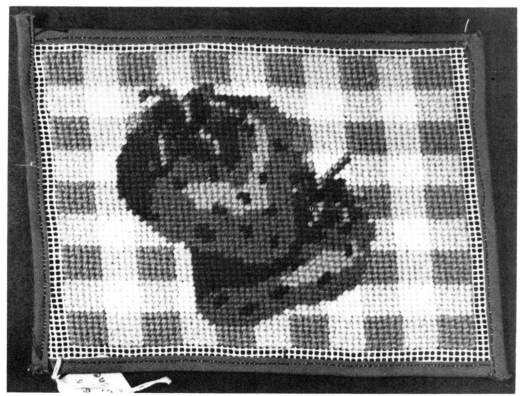

1. Look at the shape of the object.
2. Put in the darkest area, following the object's shape.
3. Put in the lightest area, following the object's shape.
4. Fill in the middle values (Figure 84).

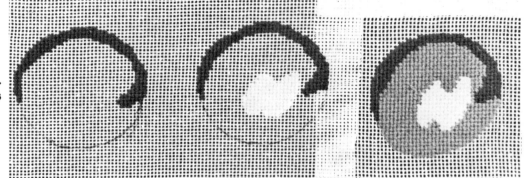

FIGURE 84.
Simple shading steps

Our next procedure (Figure 85) is scatter shading, which provides us with more realistic feeling. Our steps here are:

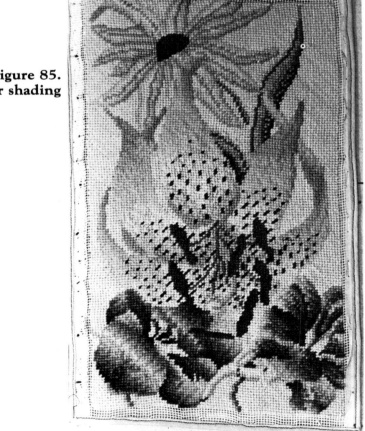

**Figure 85.
Scatter shading**

1. Determine the light and dark areas of the object.
2. Put in the dark area, following the shape of the object, but as it approaches the medium area, leave scattered black stitches and fill these in with the next value.
3. Follow the same procedure for the light areas.
4. Follow the same procedure for the medium values (Figure 86).

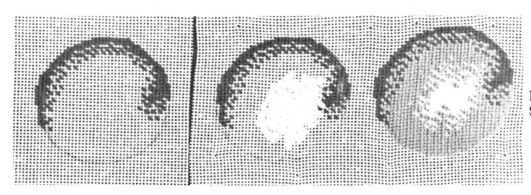

FIGURE 86.
Scatter shading steps

Our third method is the most time consuming but produces very fine, even shading that provides realism unmatched by our other procedures (Figure 87).

FIGURE 87.
Mixed and scattered shading

1. Divide the threads into three categories: light values, middle values, and dark values.
2. Determine the light, middle, and dark areas of the object, following the shape of the object.
3. Using the light threads, stitch in the center of the light area using three strands of the lightest value.
4. Stitch around this light area using two strands of the lightest value and one strand of the next value.
5. Proceed in this manner, using the following mixes, until all the light values are used:

    Three strands of the lightest (*a*)
    Two strands *a* and one strand *b*
    One strand *a* and two strands *b*
    Three strands *b*
    Two strands *b* and one strand *c*, and so on.
6. Determine where the darkest areas are and proceed as above.
7. Determine the middle-value areas and proceed as above (Figure 88).

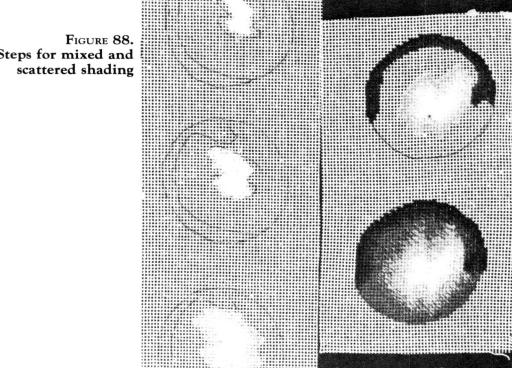

FIGURE 88.
Steps for mixed and
scattered shading

When learning to shade, it is always helpful to study photographs. Light areas are determined by where light is most intense. Look around you to study how light hits objects from various directions. As you study what happens with the light, also note whether the hues are changed by the light. Sketch them. This exercise will help you in your shading stitching.

EXERCISES

1. Take a natural object and draw it in color, noting the shading. Match the hues and values in your drawing to yarns.
2. Put the design in Exercise 1 on canvas in three different size meshes—12, 16, and 18. Stitch the size 12 in simple shading, the size 16 in scatter shading, and the size 18 in mixed and scattered shading, using the continental stitch.
3. Put the design in Exercise 1 on canvas and stitch it in a rougher stitch of your choosing, such as Scotch.

Crewel Stitches on Canvas

Almost all embroidery stitches are adaptable to canvas if you begin to think that canvas is a fabric. This opens a new door to our canvas vocabulary and allows us to make use of the multitude of stitches found in embroidery and crewel books.

The first step in adapting crewel stitches to canvas is planning. What effects do you want to achieve? Again, experimenting to achieve effects is of utmost importance.

Three questions posed by your planning will be: (1) Will the stitch employed completely cover the canvas? (2) Do I want a raised dimensional effect? and (3) Will I have to cover the canvas with a traditional background stitch before employing my crewel stitch?

Let us explore each of these questions, beginning with stitches that will completely cover the canvas.

The most common stitch that comes from the world of crewel is "long and short." Long and short provides us with marvelous shading possibilities as well as directional freedom by freeing us from adherence to the use of the holes in the canvas. Split-stitch your outline; then begin on this edge of your design area at the center and lay your beginning long and short stitches, working out to the

FIGURE 89. Long and short stitch and satin stitch

sides. Then work *into* those stitches using stitches all the same length, as shown (Figure 89). Do not worry about the canvas mesh, just work the stitch as it needs to be. Most times you will have several threads emanating from the same place.

Satin stitch also works very well in this manner and is simple to accomplish. Again, split-stitch your outlines as shown. Satin stitch is usually worked on an angle.

Another crewel technique that is most useful on canvas is couching. Couching is the attaching of cores or bundles of fibers to a fabric by using stitches over these cores or bundles to hold them in place. A variety of effects can be accomplished by determining what core to use—for example, homespun yarn, leather, raffia, feathers, or metallics. The simplest way to couch is with straight stitches. When the cores are stitched in place, the core ends are pulled or "plunged" to the reverse side with a chenille needle. Another interesting effect is to couch invisibly with sewing thread through textured fibers. Interest can also be achieved by using varied stitches to couch, such as herringbone, crosses, cretans, etc. (Figure 90). One of the joys of couching is that you are not restricted to working in straight lines; curves can be accomplished beautifully with couching (Figure 91). Experiment with pushing your fiber cores up to achieve a puffy effect as well. We note here also that couching works very well when laid on top of background stitches in narrow lines. Fine details can be achieved on a design by couching rather than resorting to very fine canvas.

FIGURE 90. Couching

FIGURE 91.
Couching in curves

Many of the crewel stitches give very raised dimensional effects, and they also work beautifully on canvas. The raised cup stitch and raised buttonhole stitch are only two of many.

The raised cup stitch is done as shown (Figures 92a and b). Keep in mind that this stitch, like all the raised stitches, provides high impact. In terms of my

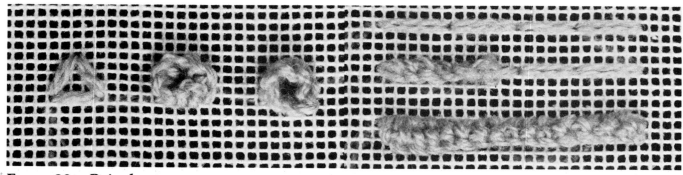

FIGURE 92a. Raised cup stitch and raised cup stitch done in a straight line

FIGURE 92b. Raised cup stitch

Buttonhole stitch over the bars only. Continue around the triangle.

Do a second row of buttonhole stitch going over only the loops of the buttonhole stitches in the first row. End by running yarn down the side of the rows, plunging to the back and securing. Do not pull tight.

texture ratings, it has a value of 6. The basics of the raised cup can be done in curved or straight lines to add dimension to areas, especially edges, and is accomplished in the manner shown. The rows of stitches can be continued and expanded as much as desired. Experiment with various effects. These stitches can be done on blank canvas as well as on background stitching (Figure 93).

FIGURE 93. Raised cup stitch used on the pine cone and for the berries

The raised buttonhole is accomplished by laying bars and buttonholing vertically over these bars as shown. The bars do not have to be in straight lines but may curve around design areas as shown (Figure 94). I have found, however, that I am more comfortable when I do not make my foundation bars very wide. When I need a wide width, I lay them in sections as in tramé. Again, experiment with what is comfortable for you.

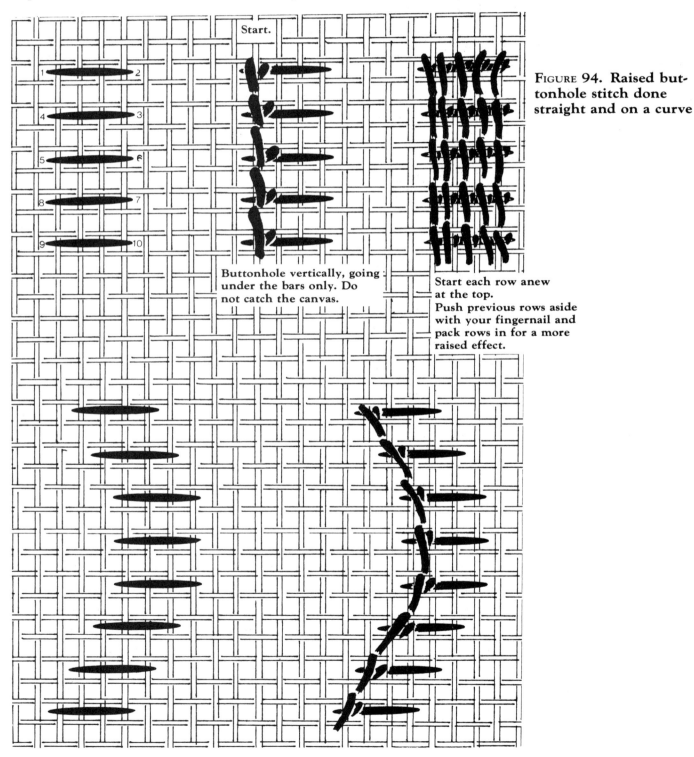

Start.

Buttonhole vertically, going under the bars only. Do not catch the canvas.

Start each row anew at the top.
Push previous rows aside with your fingernail and pack rows in for a more raised effect.

FIGURE 94. **Raised buttonhole stitch done straight and on a curve**

Try more of the raised stitches in crewel and stumpwork books, such as spiderwebs, to achieve marvelous effects.

Many crewel stitches do not cover the canvas but provide just the look we need. Here we will lay down a background canvas stitch such as tent or encroaching Gobelin and proceed to stitch on top.

Some of my favorites include detached chain stitches. These may be scattered or layered to get a fir-tree look, for instance (Figures 95a and b).

FIGURE 95a. Detached chain stitches used for a fir tree

FIGURE 95b. Detached chain stitch

The open chain stitch also allows great freedom and gives lovely effects. Open cretan is one of the most versatile of the crewel stitches and is simple to do (Figure 96).

The detached filling stitches also have wonderful effects. My favorite is the knotted buttonhole filling. When working this stitch, I do not lay the outline stitches as shown in crewel books but use my background stitch to attach fibers as shown (Figure 97). This particular stitch consists of two buttonhole stitches through each loop to form a knot. Make sure you do not catch any of the background stitching when working this except to attach it at the sides of a shape.

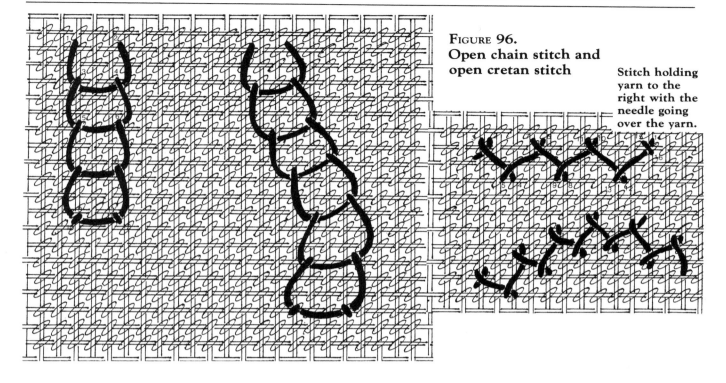

FIGURE 96.
Open chain stitch and open cretan stitch

Stitch holding yarn to the right with the needle going over the yarn.

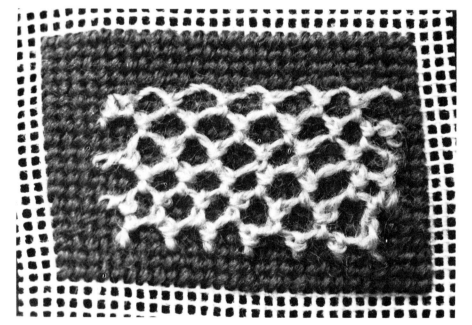

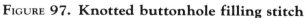

FIGURE 97. **Knotted buttonhole filling stitch**

FIGURE 98. **Deerfield embroidery design done on canvas employing crewel stitches and linen threads**

Experiment with the many other effects from the world of crewel such as stem, back stitches, and squared fillings. In fact, any crewel stitch will work on canvas; just decide first how to use it—that is, does it cover, or must it be used on top of a background stitch (Figure 98)?

Before we leave the world of crewel stitches, I would like to investigate freeing stitches. This procedure is used to construct a stitch in the correct manner but disregard its geometrics. Take, for example, the cretan stitch, shown here in its traditional and freed forms (Figure 99). The knotted buttonhole stitch also appears in this manner (Figure 100). You will notice in this stitch that instead of knotting in every loop we have skipped loops for a freed effect. Just remember, when freeing stitches, the basic construction of the stitch must be done correctly or it will not work. Therefore, practice a stitch precisely and know it before you attempt to free it.

FIGURE 99. **Open cretan stitch done traditionally and freed**

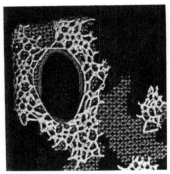

FIGURE 100. **Knotted buttonhole filling stitch freed in a design**

Experiment with freeing the stitches presented earlier in this book. Again, the stitch is constructed in the correct manner, but the geometrics of the stitch can be disregarded (Figure 101).

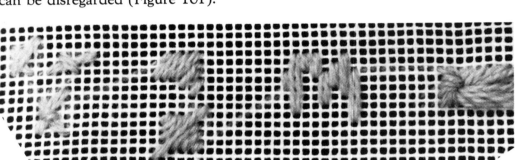

FIGURE 101. **Various stitches freed**

EXERCISES

1. Do samples of the following crewel stitches on size 12 mesh canvas: stem, satin, long and short, detached chain, cross, weaving, seeding, open cretan, coral, spider, trellis, raised buttonhole, knotted buttonhole filling. Decide whether these stitches cover or are done on top of background stitches. Samples should be two inches square.
2. Choose five different fibers and do samples of couching.
3. Choose five crewel stitches and free them on samples.
4. Choose five canvas stitches and free them on samples.
5. Make a design incorporating crewel stitches and free stitches.

Graphs

Many times, when working with canvas embroidery, it becomes more practical to work a design from a graph. This is especially true when working with geometric designs, repeat designs, plaids, lettering, and diaper patterns as well (Figure 102).

Graphing is done by counting out the design stitch by stitch onto blank canvas or by dotting each mesh of the canvas to correspond to the graph-paper squares. Each square on the graph paper is equal to one mesh on the canvas. The best graph paper to use is one with grids the same size as the canvas mesh. When this is used, the graphed designs will be the same size as the stitched canvas mesh size. When the graph paper is not the same as the canvas mesh size, count the number of threads in each direction required for the final size of the design and use the corresponding number of squares on the graph paper. Graphed designs do not have to be limited to the use of a single stitch that requires a single mesh. Almost all stitches fit into the number 24, its multiples or components.

Graphing of geometric designs is quite simple—the linear, sharp-angled qualities of these designs allow you to sketch the geometric lightly on top of the graph paper, then fill in the squares to correspond to the sketch (Figures 103a and b).

FIGURE 102. Design incorporating various types of graphing

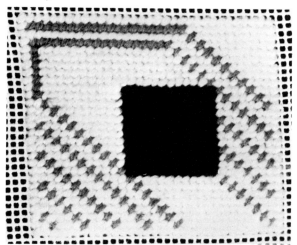

FIGURE 103a. Geometric linear design

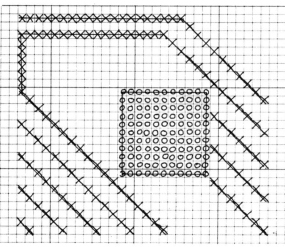

FIGURE 103b. Graph for geometric linear design

Geometric designs may also form repeat designs. One element or unit of the design is sketched onto the graph paper, then you fill in the squares to correspond to the sketch (Figures 104a and b).

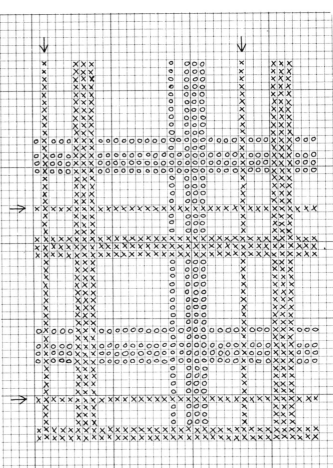

FIGURE 104a. **Plaid repeat design**

FIGURE 104b. **Graph for plaid repeat design**

Not all repeat designs are sharp angled and linear; some are based on curves. Curved designs are handled in much the same manner as the geometric designs, by lightly sketching the designs on graph paper and filling in the squares (Figures 105a and b). This type of design takes more experimentation, to get the curves to flow, than do geometric linear designs.

FIGURE 105a. Geometric design incorporating curves

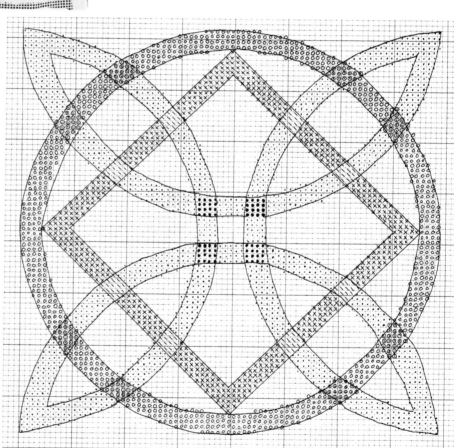

FIGURE 105b. Graph for curved geometric design

EXERCISES

1. Draw a geometric repeat design on graph paper.
2. Draw a plaid on graph paper.
3. Draw a curved repeat design on graph paper.
4. Stitch one of the above designs.

FIGURE 106.

Lettering

There are many books on lettering or calligraphy on the market today. Some of these deal entirely with needlework. All can serve as wonderful references for work with lettering. Do not limit yourself to the books alone—experiment on your own.

Curved styles of lettering as well as straight styles can easily be worked out by sketching lightly on your graph paper and then filling in the squares (Figure 106).

When working with lettering, I graph the entire message on graph paper and then cut the graph paper apart (Figure 107). The next step is to reposition it on another sheet of graph paper the finished size of the piece, making sure the graph grids line up, and taping these pieces in place (Figure 108). In this manner I am able to determine how the finished lettering will look. It is helpful to mark the centers both vertically and horizontally on the large graph-paper sheet.

FIGURE 107.
Graphed message

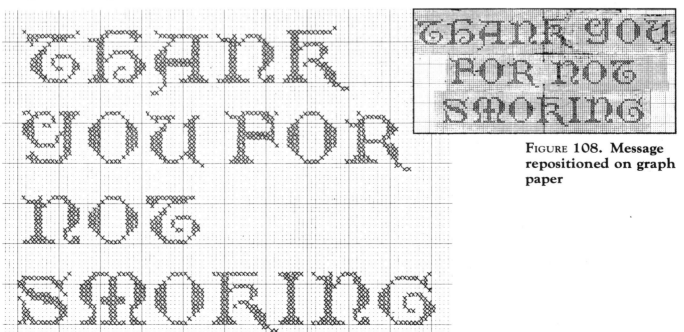

FIGURE 108. **Message repositioned on graph paper**

When your design is final on your graph paper, you can stitch onto blank canvas following this graph. I prefer to dot the lettering onto the canvas with a permanent fine-tip marking pen and then stitch (Figure 109). This method allows me the freedom of using any stitches I desire to do the lettering or design (Figure 110).

FIGURE 109. **Message dotted on canvas**

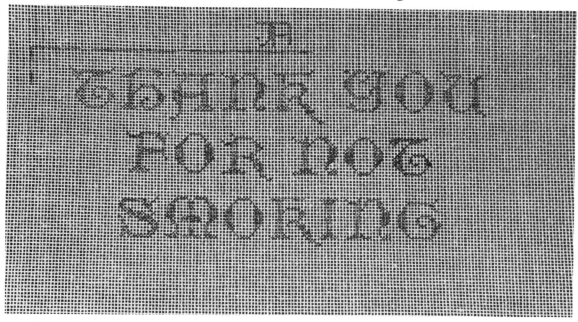

FIGURE 110. **Message stitched**

If you wish to enlarge or reduce a letter's size, you must do it from the bottom, top, and each side. In other words, one square would become four squares. In this manner the proportions of the letter are kept the same (Figure 111).

FIGURE 111. **Various letters enlarged**

EXERCISES

1. Draw on graph paper a straight alphabet and a curved alphabet. Do not copy from previously graphed designs; sketch your own.
2. Graph a message and reposition it ready to be stitched.
3. Enlarge on graph paper the two alphabets drawn for Exercise 1.
4. Stitch a design incorporating lettering.

Diaper Patterns

Repeat patterns can be formed by positioning and combining stitches. A simple example is the St. George and St. Andrew stitch. Color placement can also form repeat patterns as well (Figure 112). This combining of patterns with stitch and/or color placement is called diaper patterning. The term *diaper pattern* is most commonly derived from weaving, where it is defined as a one-inch repeat. However, we also find patterning in architecture, ironwork, and mosaics, to mention but a few sources. The effectiveness of diaper patterns is greatly influenced by combining textures and colors.

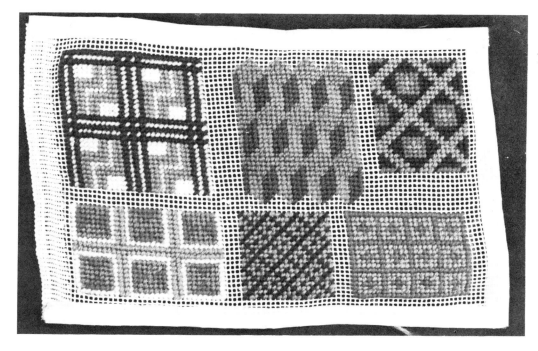

FIGURE 112.

Experimentation is of the essence here, and graph paper can be a big help (Figure 113).

Diaper patterns can be made to fit into a design area by compensating the stitch parts as we would compensate any stitch (Figure 114).

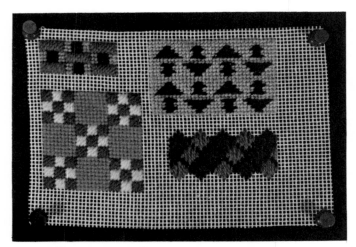

FIGURE 113. **Diaper patterns incorporating various stitches**

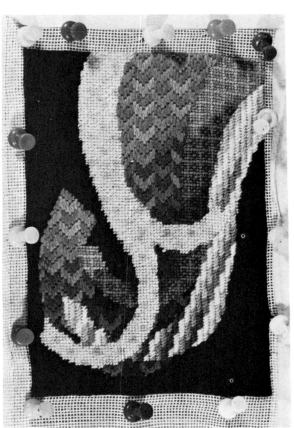

FIGURE 114. **"Hair," stitched design incorporating diaper patterns, by the author**

EXERCISES

1. Develop a diaper pattern on graph paper, using color only to form the pattern. Stitch at least a three-inch-square sample of your design, using the tent stitch.
2. Develop a diaper pattern on graph paper using different stitches and colors to form the pattern. Stitch at least a three-inch-square sample of this pattern.
3. Develop two diaper patterns, one incorporating only one stitch and the other employing different stitches. Stitch these two patterns into a design shape such as an oval, circle, or free form.

Borders

At times we wish to border our designs but are confused about how to handle them. The best procedure is actually to draw in a border as you did with the rest of the design to see if it works. It is a very important part of the overall design and has a great impact. Disaster occurs when a design is stitched and a border is "added."

Some of the ways borders can be achieved follow:

1. Turning corners with a design. Our design units may follow along the way they sit when they reach a corner, or they may be angled or mitered (Figure 115).

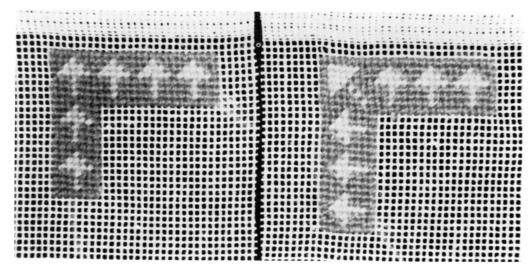

FIGURE 115.

2. Using only one stitch to form a border. Here the stitch follows the border area and is filled in. The one stitch can also be mitered at the corners to give another effect (Figure 116). When mitering, we must find the diagonals at the corners and have the stitch angles meet at the diagonal.

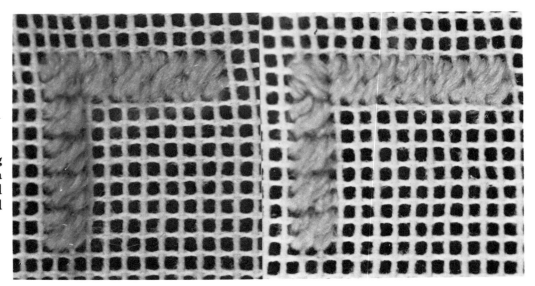

FIGURE 116. Using one stitch to form a border as it sits and mitered

3. Combining various stitches for texture in a border. This type of border can also incorporate diaper patterns, and they can follow in straight or sitting form or be angled or mitered (Figure 117).

FIGURE 117. Textured border as it sits and mitered

Borders are most successful when they are graphed. I usually work from the center of *each* side out to the corners. This, however, does not mean that your filling in of your experimental charts requires your graphing the entire piece. Graph from the center to the corner horizontally and from one vertical side to the same corner (Figure 118). In this manner you will have one quarter or quadrant of your border worked out. Then just flop it over to have it coincide with the remaining three quadrants. Some of the difficulty can be eliminated when mitering corners if a small pocket mirror is placed at the diagonal of the stitch chart. The resulting image on the mirror is the mitering and can be charted from the mirror (Figure 119).

Border patterning need not be restricted to the borders of a design; it can function within a design or form an entire design (Figure 120). As with all canvaswork techniques, experiment and explore the possibilities.

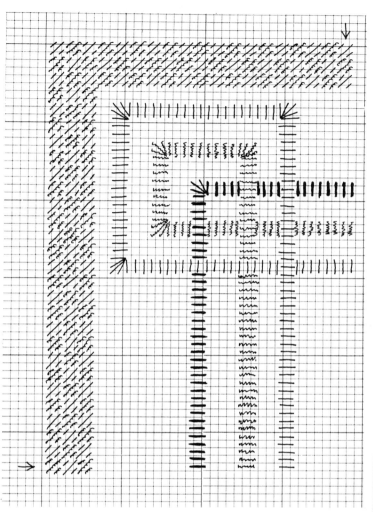

FIGURE 118. One quadrant of a border
graphed

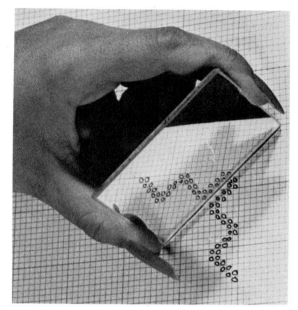

FIGURE 119. Use of a pocket mirror to miter a border corner

FIGURE 120. Stitched border design

EXERCISES

1. Graph and stitch a border using a design sitting and mitered.
2. Graph and stitch borders using only one stitch from each of the following stitch families: cross, continental, Scotch, Gobelin, oblique, star, bargello, couching.
3. Graph and stitch a border combining several stitches sitting and mitered.
4. Stitch a design that incorporates a border within the design.
5. Stitch a design that is composed solely of borders.
6. Stitch a design that has a border surrounding it.

Bargello and Hungarian Point

Bargello or Florentine canvaswork is very simply defined as the patterning of stitches, usually upright ones, in colors or values. These patternings can be put into two basic categories: flame and Hungarian point (Figure 121).

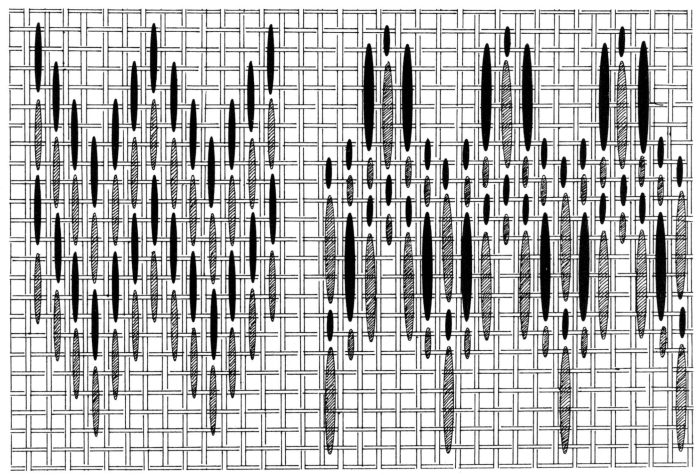

FIGURE 121. Flame pattern (*left*) and Hungarian point pattern

The flame patterns are formed by color and the movement or steps the stitch takes as it is worked. Many books on the subject are available, most including instructions that read "4 step 2, 3 step 1," etc. By "4 step 2" we mean that each vertical stitch would cover four horizontal threads and the stitch next to it would also cover four threads but is started two horizontal threads above or below it. Effects can be changed greatly by varying the stepping (Figure 122).

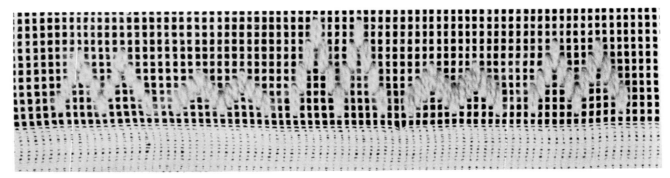

FIGURE 122. **Effects of changing stepping in flame patterns**

The Hungarian point patterns are also varied by stepping, but in this case we are working with the Hungarian stitch and stepping long and short stitches to form patterns. This combination of pattern and texture will result in a brocade effect. The long stitches for Hungarian point can vary from going over four to ten vertical threads, but the short stitches are usually stitched over two vertical threads (Figure 123).

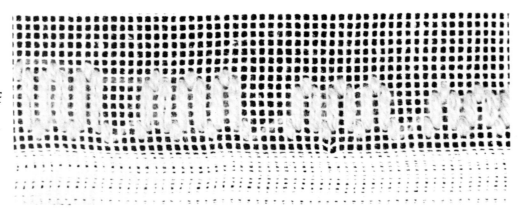

FIGURE 123. **Effects of changing stepping in Hungarian point patterns**

One of the joys of this type of stitching is developing your own designs. The procedures are simple and very satisfying. The first step is to pick a color scheme. One simple way to see how your fiber colors will appear is to wind threads around a piece of cardboard or a pencil so that the threads touch each other. In this manner you can ascertain approximately what the color relationships will be and the order in which the colors will be used (Figure 124).

Second, decide what type of patterning to use: flame or Hungarian point. Now take graph paper and colored pencils in your design colors and fill in each square on the paper as one thread to be covered. Work with these patternings until you develop one that pleases you. Then try a small portion of the pattern on your canvas to see if it still pleases you (Figure 125). This is the point where patterns and colors can be changed.

FIGURE 124. **Various colors of yarns wound to see color relationships**

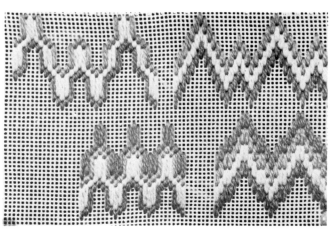

FIGURE 125. **Doodle cloth of graphed patterns stitched**

The piece is now ready to be stitched. I find that bargello is best worked on size 14 canvas, but you are not restricted to this. Just be very careful that your canvas is covered. Start at the center of the canvas or design area and work out to the sides (Figure 126). It is imperative that these patterns be worked into the stitch previously done to obtain coverage and wearability. Also remember to pick up a bit of the fiber of the previous stitch as you work.

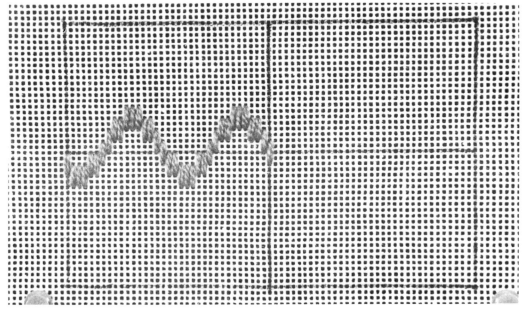

FIGURE 126. **Start at the center and work out to the sides.**

An easy way to keep track of your fibers is to loop them around a yarn holder. Commercial ones are available in stores, or you can use plastic bottle or can holders that surround soda or beer cans. If you loop the yarn through each hole in an overhand knot or half hitch, the yarn can be removed strand by strand instead of untying each time a new strand is needed.

We are not restricted to doing our bargello designs in precise patterns row upon row. Experimentation can be done with changing the length and stepping of patterns to give an interesting effect (Figure 127). Combining patterns in a patchwork using the same colors also gives interest (Figure 128). Sometimes I draw a light freehand curve or line on my graph paper and use this as a guide for my patterning (Figures 129a and b).

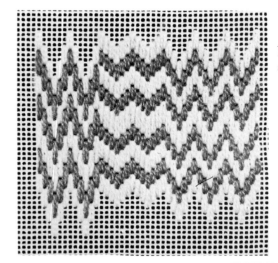

FIGURE 127. **Changing stepping within an area**

FIGURE 128. **Combining patterns to form a patchwork**

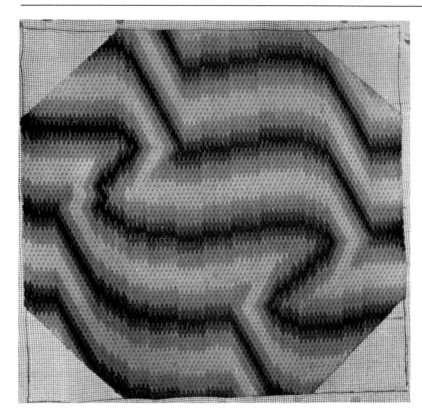

FIGURE 129a. Bargello developed from a freely drawn line

FIGURE 129b.
Graph for freely drawn pattern

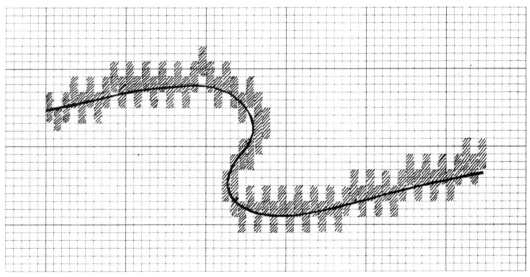

EXERCISES

1. Develop on graph paper and stitch samples of three different flame patterns.
2. Develop on graph paper and stitch samples of three different Hungarian point patterns.
3. Stitch a freely sketched pattern.

Radiating Bargello

Another delightful way to handle bargello patterns is to turn to the basic design form of radiating lines. Many books use the term *four-way bargello* for this type of patterning.

We have two ways of handling this form of patterning:

1. Starting from the center of the point of radiation, first find the center of the graph paper or, if you want to work on blank canvas, the center of the canvas. The center is always a "hole" of the canvas. Then mark the diagonals with sewing thread or a permanent marker on canvas or a pencil line on graph paper (Figure 130). Then stitch or graph your pattern for one quadrant and turn your pattern 90 degrees when the diagonal is reached (Figure 131). The vertical stitches will form right angles as they meet on each diagonal (Figure 132).

FIGURE 130.
Diagonals marked on graph paper

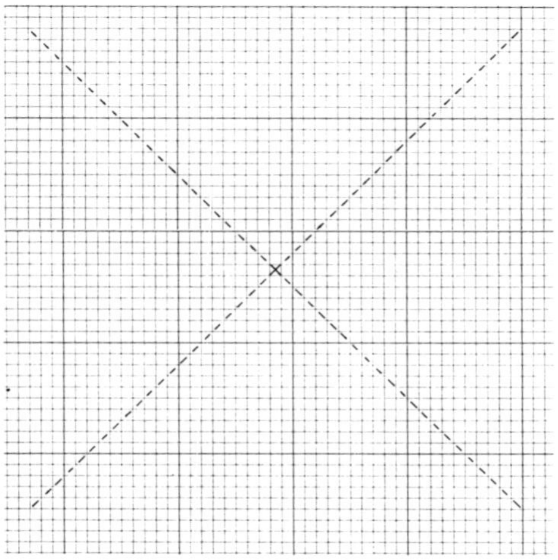

FIGURE 131.
Two quadrants graphed

FIGURE 132.
Four quadrants stitched

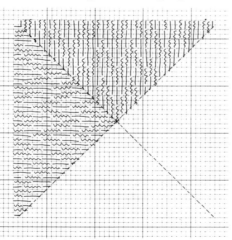

2. Working from the outer edges to the center, we mark our diagonals as before and begin working from the center of the outer edge. A pattern may be lightly sketched with pencil and then formed for the quadrant, or it may be precisely graphed in (Figure 133). Another way to work is to take paper the size of the finished area and fold it into quadrants (much the same way as we folded paper to make snowflakes as children). Then cut this folded paper into a paper pattern. Unfold and trace the resulting pattern onto your graph paper or canvas in one quadrant (Figure 134) and proceed as above.

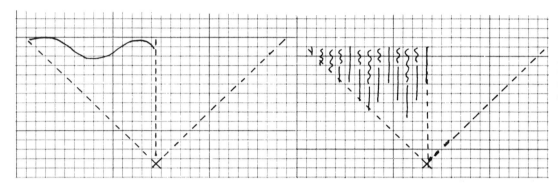

FIGURE 133. Sketch line for first quadrant and graph for half the first quadrant

FIGURE 134. Folded-paper design steps

Interesting patterns and effects can be achieved by taking small radiating patterns and isolating them (Figure 135). These can also be repeated to form diaper patterns (Figure 136). Radiating bargellos also gain impact when the center is changed to another place in the design area (Figure 137). Experiment with freeing the centers, having radiating patterns overlap (Figure 138), or using freely drawn lines (Figure 139).

FIGURE 135. **Isolated radiating patterns**

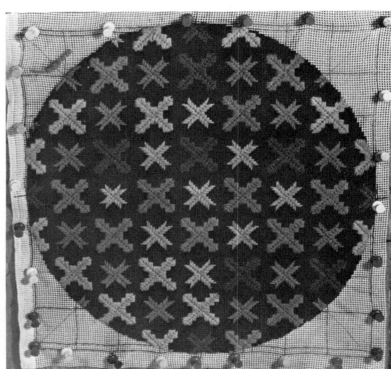

FIGURE 136. **Diaper pattern of radiating bargellos**

FIGURE 137. **Off-center design**

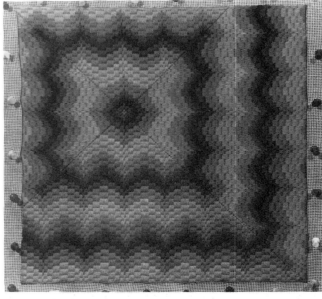

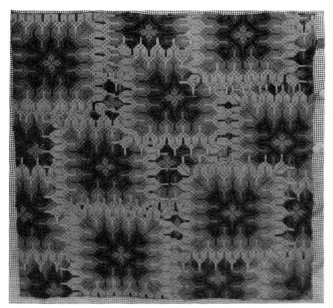

FIGURE 138. **Overlapping designs**

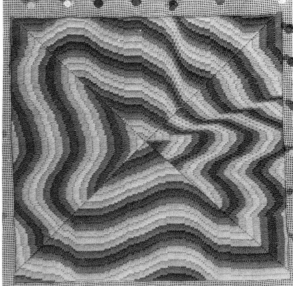

FIGURE 139. **Freely drawn design**

EXERCISES

1. Design on graph paper a radiating bargello starting at the center and working out.
2. Design on graph paper a radiating bargello starting at the outer edge.
3. Design on graph paper a radiating bargello using the folded-paper method.
4. Draw a design incorporating an isolated radiating pattern.
5. Design on graph paper a diaper pattern using radiating bargello patterns.
6. Design and stitch a radiating bargello pattern that is off-center.
7. Design and stitch a design using overlapping radiating bargellos.
8. Design and stitch a freely drawn radiating bargello.

Bargello in Shapes and Shading

FIGURE 140. "Dragon" in shaded bargello patterning by the author, from the private collection of Dr. and Mrs. B. Shapiro, Livingston, N. J.

Bargello patterning becomes very effective when put into shapes rather than just doing patterns in squares of rectangles, which we are most familiar with (Figure 140). Some suggestions here will help make your exploration a bit easier. The types of designs you use cannot be very finely detailed. The shapes must be rather open, without narrow or sharp-pointed edges.

After your design is drawn in black and white, choose your pattern and color. When choosing your pattern, nature provides the best inspiration. A photo of the object will help lead you to your patterning with a great deal of ease (Figure 141). Colors are chosen in the same manner as with all bargellos and are tried out in the same way as well. I usually find the center of a shape and stitch or chart out to the sides (Figure 142).

FIGURE 141. **Pineapple as a pattern inspiration**

FIGURE 142. **Begin at the center and work out to the sides.**

FIGURE 143. **"Fruits," shaded bargello shapes, by the author**

To give form to an object, you can shade your bargello shapes in much the same manner we shade any canvaswork (Figure 143). Determine the light and dark areas of the design object, then categorize your fibers by choosing values for each color of your bargello color scheme.

Start stitching your bargello pattern in the center of the darkest area of your shape, using the darkest value of each color desired. Switch to the next values of your colors and stitch, keeping the pattern the same. Proceed with the changing values, but keep the pattern constant until your area is shaded as you desire (Figure 144).

FIGURE 144. **Steps to shading fish in bargello patterning**

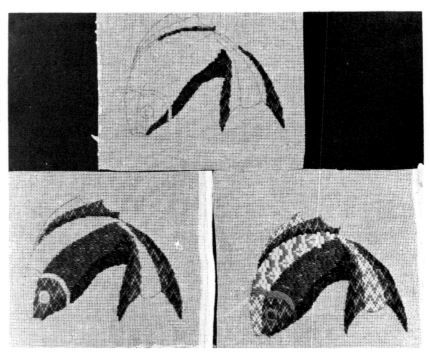

This procedure is time consuming and care must be taken to keep the pattern flowing and the colors and values of the fibers in order, but it is well worth the effort to achieve the form that results.

EXERCISES

1. Draw a design incorporating bargello designs in shapes. Choose bargello patterns for each shape and stitch the design.
2. Shade a natural object in bargello patterning.

Lost Canvas

Canvas embroidery stitches need not be limited to canvas; fabrics can also be a foundation for canvas-type stitches.

When a fabric is not an even-weave, we use a method called "lost canvas" or "waste canvas" (Figure 145). The steps are as follows:

FIGURE 145.
Lost-canvas designs on neckties

1. Put the design on a lightweight canvas. Cross-stitch canvas works very well. Do not use interlock canvas, only mono or penelope.
2. Baste the design on the canvas to the fabric background, using sewing thread.

117

3. Stitch through both the canvas and the fabric, using a pointed needle. Crewel needles work best. Stitching is accomplished easily if the work is done on a frame. Make sure that you do not catch any of the canvas threads.
4. When the stitching is completed, pull the canvas threads out, one at a time, using tweezers. It helps to dampen the canvas slightly to ease the pulling out of the threads (Figure 146).

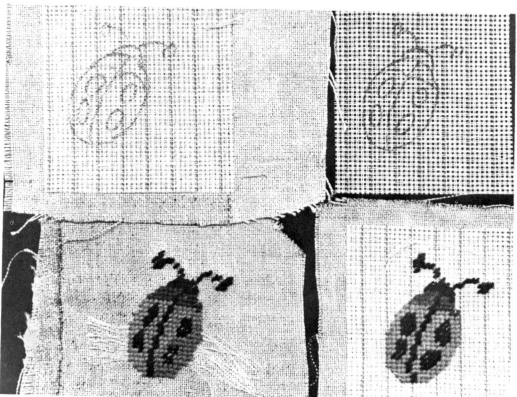

FIGURE 146. Steps for lost canvas on textiles

Any fabric can be used for this technique if some thought is given to its construction. Homespuns, wools, cottons, and heavy-to-medium-weight fabrics need no special handling for lost canvas work. Lightweight, fragile, and tightly woven fabrics such as silk, organdy, and knits are more easily handled in lost canvas work if it is backed or lined with a firm fiber such as muslin before stitching. This will prevent puckering and shredding and keep the underneath threads on sheer fabrics from showing through to the front. Baste this lining to the fabric by laying it flat and basting through the centers horizontally, vertically, and diagonally. Then baste the canvas to the fabric and proceed as in the above steps (Figure 147).

The lost canvas technique can also be used on canvas when very fine detail is desired, as when adding eyes to a face. The same steps as were used on fabric are followed, but the canvas beneath is usually stitched and then the lost canvas design basted on and stitched through, using a crewel needle (Figure 148).

FIGURE 147. **Lining a knit for lost-canvas work**

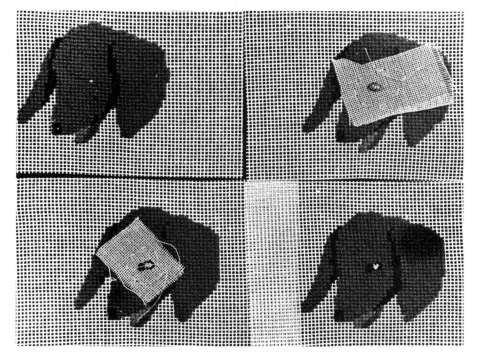

FIGURE 148. **Steps for lost-canvas work on canvas**

EXERCISES

1. Do an example of lost canvas technique on a fabric that does not require lining.
2. Do an example of lost canvas technique on a knit fabric and a sheer fabric, both of which require lining.
3. Do an example of lost canvas technique on previously stitched canvas-work.

Canvas Stitches on Fabric

Fabrics that are even-weave lend themselves to canvas embroidery by the very fact that they *are* even-weave, as is canvas. Even-weave fabrics are those with threads spaced equidistant both horizontally and vertically. These fabrics can be found among the many available in your sewing fabric store. Using a six-inch rule on fabrics when you go shopping will help you purchase an even-weave. Just count the number of threads to the inch horizontally and then do the same vertically. If the number is the same, the fabric is an even-weave.

Needlework stores also carry even-weave fabrics. They are known as even-weave or counted thread fabrics and are woven in two basic types: hardanger and aida cloth. The popularity of the counted thread types of embroideries has now made these fabrics available in a variety of mesh sizes and colors (Figure 149).

FIGURE 149. Hardanger (*left*) and aida cloths

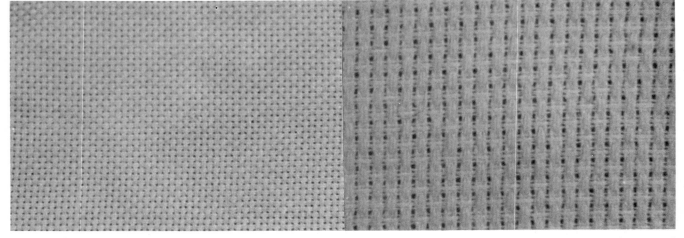

Stitching is done in the same manner as on canvas, but the background does not have to be entirely filled in. Vary the types of yarns by thickness and content to add interest. I prefer to use a tapestry needle on these fabrics, and I work on a frame.

Application of your design requires some care. The light-box method or the tissue-paper method of applying designs both work well. I prefer to trace the design onto tulle using a black permanent marker. The tulle is then placed on the fabric and the design is traced again through the tulle onto the fabric. I have also found that a gray nonwaterproof fine-tip marker works well, and there is now available a pen with ink that washes out of the fabric. Do not paint in your designs but rather keep the design on the fabric in outline form and refer to your drawing of your design as you work (Figure 150).

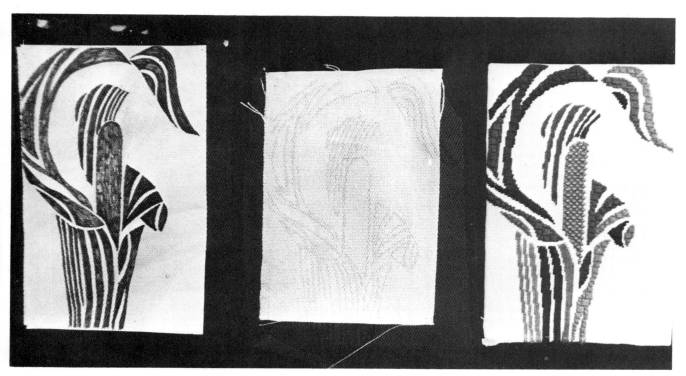

FIGURE 150. **Procedure for putting designs on even-weave textiles**

EXERCISES

1. Collect examples of even-weave fabrics and mark the mesh size for each.
2. Draw a design and apply it to an even-weave fabric and stitch it, using traditional canvas embroidery stitches and at least two different types of yarns.

Drawn
Fabric on Canvas

Among the vast array of fabric techniques in the world of embroidery that lend themselves perfectly to canvas is drawn fabric work. Its other labels are "pulled thread" or "pulled work." The basic principle of this technique is to compress stitches tightly so that the warp and weft form designs with the holes (Figure 151). The result is an open, lacy effect.

FIGURE 151. "Wedding Rings," drawn fabric design, by the author

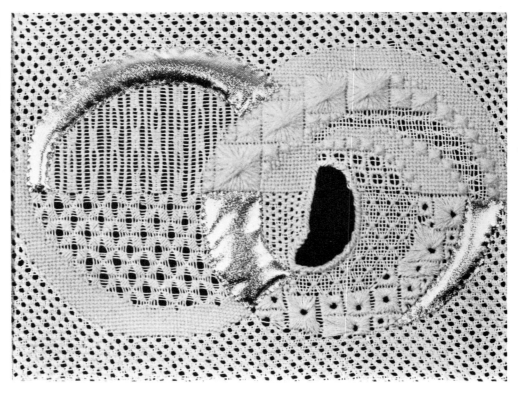

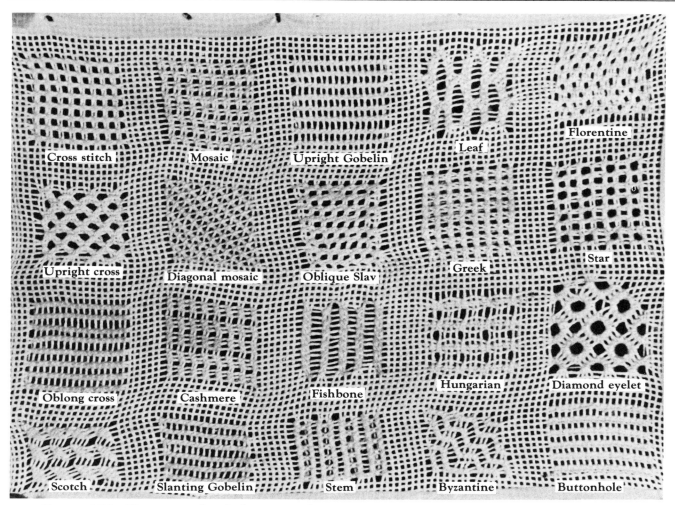

Cross stitch · Mosaic · Upright Gobelin · Leaf · Florentine

Upright cross · Diagonal mosaic · Oblique Slav · Greek · Star

Oblong cross · Cashmere · Fishbone · Hungarian · Diamond eyelet

Scotch · Slanting Gobelin · Stem · Byzantine · Buttonhole

FIGURE **152. Canvaswork stitches tensed**

Essentially any of the stitches traditionally used for drawn fabric work can be used on canvas, which is after all a textile. Also play with those stitches traditionally used only for canvaswork (Figure 152). The most pleasing effects are obtained when the thread used is the same color as the canvas. In this way the patterns formed become the most prominent. Some very interesting effects can be obtained, however, by using colored fibers. The canvas can also be colored by painting it with acrylic paints or painting on cold-water dyes. When using dyes, make sure that you have made the dyed area fast.

This technique works best on mono-canvas. Penelope can also be used, but the effect is not as clean-cut. I also find a frame useful, since the canvas is very easily distorted with this technique.

The best way to begin is with a waste knot in a straight line. The stitches can be tensed very tightly or a bit loosely to obtain different effects (Figure 153). At the end of the row, go over the last step of a stitch twice, to secure the tensing. The thread is ended off in a straight line on the back of the work. I find that a pointed needle is useful when ending off.

FIGURE **153. Three degrees of tensing: loose (*top*), medium (*middle*), tight (*bottom*)**

Weak yarns do not work well for drawn fabric work because of the stress of pulling. Crochet threads, linens, perle cotton (sizes 5 and 8), and strong, high-quality wools seem to work the best. Here again, experiment with fibers to see what happens.

The impact of drawn fabric areas is very high, so much thought should be given to how these areas will function in a piece of canvaswork as well as the hues of the material the piece is to be mounted on.

EXERCISES

1. Do one-inch squares of drawn fabric technique using at least twelve different stitches on size 14, 16, and 18 mono-canvas. Vary the tensing of the stitches on each sample.
2. Design and stitch a canvaswork piece incorporating drawn fabric technique.
3. Design and stitch a canvaswork piece incorporating drawn fabric technique using colored yarns.

Needleweaving

Needleweaving as a type of embroidery is more than three thousand years old and is actually a form of darning. Because needleweaving in traditional embroideries has always been very successful worked on plain, coarsely woven textiles, canvas becomes an excellent medium both for traditional and contemporary work. Fibers used for needleweaving can be varied as the design requires. The traditional wools, silks, and cottons may be used as well as raffia, string, and wire (Figure 154).

The technique can be accomplished in a variety of ways: on top of canvas, with weft threads drawn out, and by drawing out threads to form layers. Other forms of embroidery that use the withdrawing of threads can also work, such as hardanger (Figure 155).

FIGURE 154. "The Fourth Day," design incorporating needleweaving, by the author

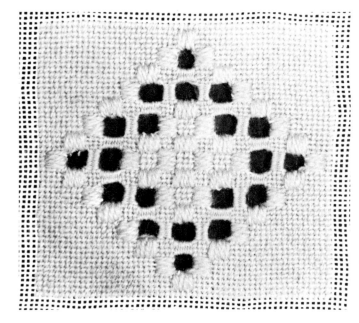

FIGURE 155. Hardanger on canvas

125

The basic stitch used is the traditional needleweaving one. However, experimentation will show that any stitch that can be wrapped around and that covers the warps will work very well, such as buttonhole or cretan as well as weaving over and under (tabby weave) a number of warps (Figure 156). The traditional needleweaving stitch is basically an over-and-under action. Bring the needle over the right warp and under the left, up and over the left and under the right, back over, and proceed from the beginning. This will give you a figure-eight action. Push the stitches up as you work so that the warp is completely covered (Figures 157a and b).

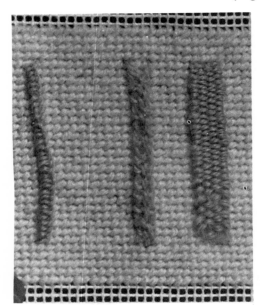

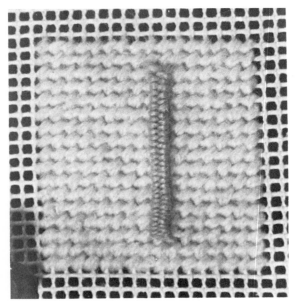

FIGURE 156. Needle-weaving using button-hole (*left*), cretan, and tabby weave

FIGURE 157a (*above, center*). Traditional needleweaving

FIGURE 157b (*above, right*). Traditional needleweaving stitch

When needleweaving is worked on top of canvas, the canvas is worked in a background stitch and warp threads are laid on top of this ground (Figure 158). Any type of canvas can be used. These warp threads are then woven, using the method desired. The warps can be laid very symmetrically or freely and randomly. Bundled warps in groups can be woven around as well and form

FIGURE 158. Pine needles done in needleweaving on top of a canvas back-ground

FIGURE 159. Needle-weaving in bundles with random warps

interesting patterns (Figure 159). Additional warps can be laid down on top of the completed needleweaving and woven to give built-up effects.

You are not limited to using only threads on top of canvas. Dimension can be added by using wire and shaping it into forms and needleweaving. When using wire as warp, florists' wire (the kind used for beaded flowers) works very well. Twist the wires together on the reverse side of the work to hold firmly or run double the desired length through and bring them up to form double warps (Figure 160). When working with wire on top of canvas it is not necessary to have the wire warp attached at both ends; one end can hang free. When this is done, the wire is looped in a horseshoe shape and then needlewoven, starting at the top and needleweaving around the loose end of yarn and the wires (Figure 161).

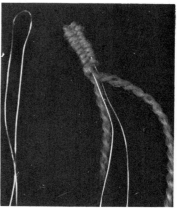

FIGURE 161. Needleweaving over wires that hang free

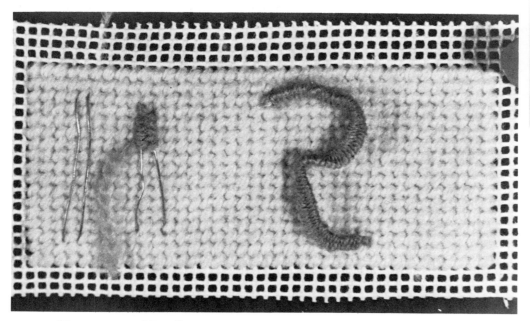

FIGURE 160. Needleweaving over wire

The basic steps to needleweaving on top of canvas are:

1. Lay the warp threads.
2. Come up through the background near the right warp.
3. Needleweave (using a tapestry needle). Do not put the needle through the background except to begin and end.
4. When completed, bring needle to the rear and end off.

To change colors, weave through the back of the weaving carefully and snip off, using a pointed needle to make the ending more efficient.

Needleweaving when weft threads are withdrawn produces interesting patterns as well as shadows behind the areas that are needlewoven. Needless to say, because of the openness of the needleweaving, the underneath backing must be chosen carefully. The lighter the value of the fabric underneath these areas, the greater the shadows produced (Figure 162). Mirrors and other types of materials may also be used underneath these open areas.

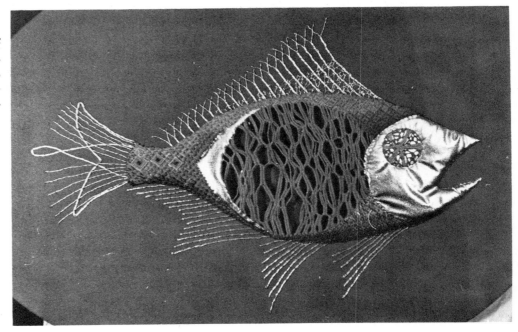

FIGURE 162. "Fillet of Fish," appliquéd canvas design incorporating needleweaving, by the author

Stitch the surrounding area of the canvas, leaving the needlewoven portion blank. Use only mono or penelope canvas for this. Remove the weft threads and then needleweave over the remaining threads in the manner you desire. Again, you are not limited to pairs of warps but can form patterns freely, using varying bundles of warp threads.

1. Stitch surrounding area (this works best if it is not edged in an upright stitch).
2. Snip weft threads in the center and unweave.
3. Weave weft threads into the reverse side of the background. If the weft threads are too short to weave, overcast them to the back of the work with sewing thread.
4. Bring the weaving fiber up through the background and weave over the canvas warp threads that remain (Figure 163).

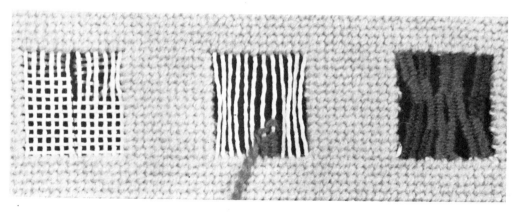

FIGURE **163.** Needle-weaving **with canvas threads withdrawn**

In order to needleweave in layers, every other weft thread is snipped and withdrawn. When this is completed, you will have three layers of threads left. Snip the bottom layer of threads, which will leave two layers to be needlewoven in any manner you choose (Figure 164). This procedure works best on mono-canvas.

The basic steps to withdrawing threads to form layers are as follows:

1. Stitch surrounding area (this works best if it is not edged in an upright stitch).
2. Snip every other weft thread from the center and unweave.
3. Weave these threads into the reverse side of the background. If the weft threads are too short to weave, overcast them to the back of the work with sewing thread.
4. Snip only the bottom layer of the three layers left from the center.
5. Follow Step 3.
6. Needleweave the remaining layers one at a time. Because needleweaving is reversible, I usually needleweave the top layer and then turn the piece over and needleweave the bottom layer from the back side of the piece (Figure 165).

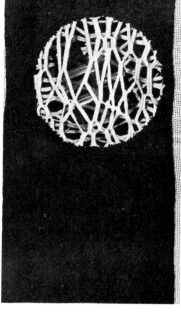

FIGURE **164.** "**The First Day,**" **needleweaving in two layers, by the author**

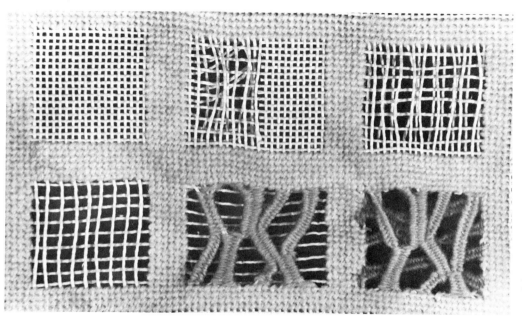

FIGURE **165. Steps for needleweaving two layers**

Experiment with not snipping that bottom layer, and needleweave using the three layers.

When needleweaving is used in canvas embroidery, preplanning is a must. These techniques, especially withdrawing threads, give a tremendous impact to the piece. The methods we discussed in texture concerning impact should be carefully applied, and sketching needlewoven areas on your designs is important. When designing, I very often shred out the areas of paper where needleweaving is to be done to see what the effect will be (Figure 166).

FIGURE 166. Paper diagrams with needlewoven area shredded

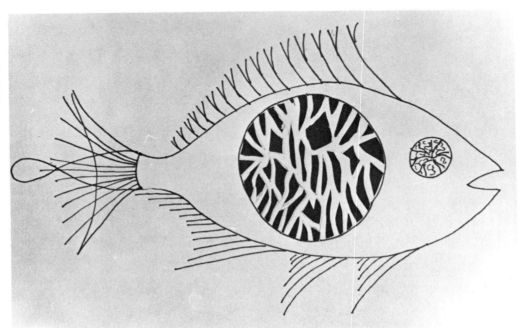

EXERCISES

1. Do one-inch samples of needleweaving using at least three different stitches other than the traditional needleweaving stitch.
2. Design and stitch a canvaswork piece employing needlework on top of canvas.
3. Design and stitch a canvaswork piece employing needleweaving using wires.
4. Design and stitch a canvaswork piece employing needleweaving with canvas threads withdrawn.

Appliqué

Appliqué by definition is the addition of one fabric to another. In canvas embroidery this may mean combining two sizes of canvas or applying canvas to fabric or conversely fabric to canvas. Appliqué allows us freedom in detail and dimension (Figure 167).

FIGURE 167. Design with balloon and basket appliquéd, by the author

Careful planning is required when using this technique, especially in regard to the shapes to be used. Very tiny areas will be quite difficult to handle, as will large ones. Shapes that are quite detailed also present special problems that must be dealt with before work begins. Smooth shapes such as mushroom tops can be handled rather simply if you remember always to leave at least three inches of shredding canvas surrounding the shape. More detailed shapes such as flower petals require about six inches of shredding canvas. This extra canvas is used to pull through in areas that do not have enough canvas (Figure 168).

Figure 168. Canvas threads pulled through for added length

The threads are pulled through to give a weaving length. I usually pull the threads through an area of this nature and then snip them in the center. Pull through very gently. Make sure that the canvas threads are not completely pulled out. Most objects to be appliquéd should be blocked before they are shredded and put on canvas or fabric. I find I am most comfortable working with the background canvas or fabric on a frame when appliquéing.

When tracing my designs to be applied, I find that when I desire a rounded effect, I make the shape very slightly larger; for a flat effect, I make it just slightly smaller.

The following are the steps for the various forms of appliqué:

APPLIQUÉ WEAVING THROUGH STITCHES
(Rounded Effect)   *(Figure 169)*

This procedure is used when the background stitch covers the back of the canvas well.

1. Stitch to the outline edge of the background canvas.
2. Stitch object on mono or penelope canvas. (If an upright, loose, etc., stitch is used, tent-stitch two rows of outline first.)
3. Unravel canvas to stitching.

Figure 169. "Mushroom Fantasy," appliqué weaving through stitches design and stitched, by the author

4. Pull two threads on all four sides of the object through the background canvas one at a time, pointing your needle in toward the center.
5. Pull the remaining threads through one at a time, pointing the needle in.
6. Weave canvas threads through the back of the stitching to anchor. Pull tightly when finished, and a rounded effect will appear (Figure 170).

FIGURE 170. **Steps for appliqué weaving through stitches (rounded effect)**

APPLIQUÉ WEAVING THROUGH STITCHES
(Flat Effect)

This procedure is used when the background stitch covers the back of the canvas well.

1. Stitch to outline edge of background canvas.
2. Stitch object on mono or penelope canvas. (If an upright, loose, etc., stitch is used, tent-stitch two rows of outline first.)
3. Unravel canvas to stitching.
4. Pin object flat onto the canvas. If the area is large or unusually detailed in shape, baste it to the canvas.

5. Pull two threads on each of the four sides through the background canvas one at a time, pointing the needle out.
6. Pull the remaining threads through one at a time, pointing the needle out.
7. Weave canvas threads through the back of the stitching in order to anchor. Pull threads until object lies flat (Figure 171).

FIGURE 171. **Steps for appliqué weaving through stitches (flat effect)**

WEAVING THROUGH CANVAS *(Rounded Effect)*

This procedure is used when the background stitch will not cover the back canvas well (herringbone, couching, etc.).

1. Stitch the object on mono or penelope canvas. (If an upright, loose, etc., stitch is used, tent-stitch two rows of outline first.)
2. Unravel to stitching.
3. Pull two threads on each of the four sides through one at a time at a point slightly inside the outline, pointing the needle in.
4. Pull the remaining threads through the canvas at a place slightly inside the outline, one at a time, pointing the needle in.
5. Weave the threads through the canvas one at a time. Pull tightly when finished, and a rounded effect will appear.
6. Finish stitching the background of the piece (Figure 172).

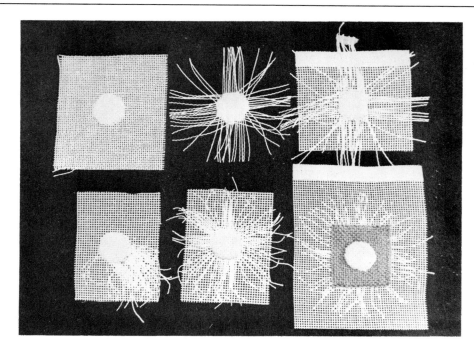

FIGURE 172. Steps for weaving through canvas (rounded effect)

WEAVING THROUGH CANVAS *(Flat Effect)*

This technique is used when the background stitch will not cover the back of the canvas well (herringbone, couching, etc.).

1. Stitch the object on mono or penelope canvas. (If an upright, loose, etc., stitch is used, tent-stitch two rows of outline first.)
2. Unravel to the stitching.
3. Pin object flat onto the canvas. If the area is large or unusually detailed in shape, baste it to the canvas.
4. Pull two threads on each of the four sides through one at a time at a point slightly outside the outline, pointing the needle out.
5. Pull threads through canvas one at a time at a point slightly outside the outline, pointing the needle slightly out.
6. Weave threads through canvas one at a time. Pull tightly when finished until object lies flat.
7. Finish-stitch the background of the piece (Figure 173).

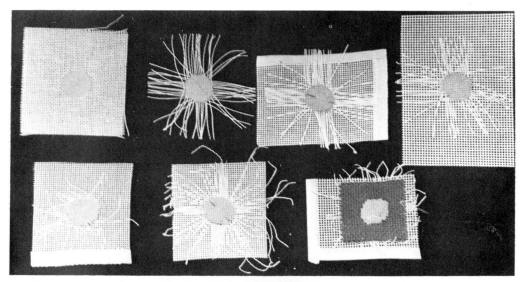

FIGURE 173. Steps for weaving through canvas (flat effect)

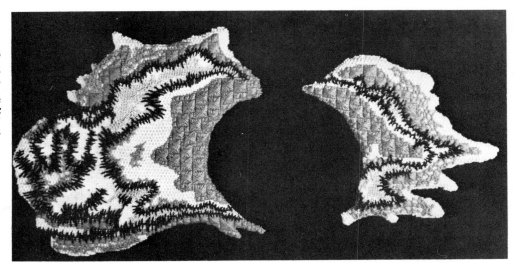

FIGURE 174. "Sun's Corona," canvas design appliquéd to fabric, by the author, from the private collection of Emily Nicholson

CANVAS TO FABRIC *(Figure 174)*

Fabrics for this procedure must be chosen with care. Firm fabrics work very well; however, silks and very loosely woven fabrics require a firm fabric such as linen or muslin placed behind them so that the fabrics hold up. Baste the lining fabric and the background fabric together and appliqué the canvas through both. A frame is a necessity for this procedure.

1. Stitch the object on mono or penelope canvas. (If an upright, loose, etc., stitch is used, tent-stitch two rows of outline first.)
2. Unravel canvas to the stitching.
3. Pull two threads on each of the four sides through one at a time to obtain either a flat or rounded effect.
4. Pull remaining threads through fabric one at a time to obtain either a rounded or flat effect.
5. Tie tightly, in square knots, pairs of canvas threads on the reverse side (Figure 175).

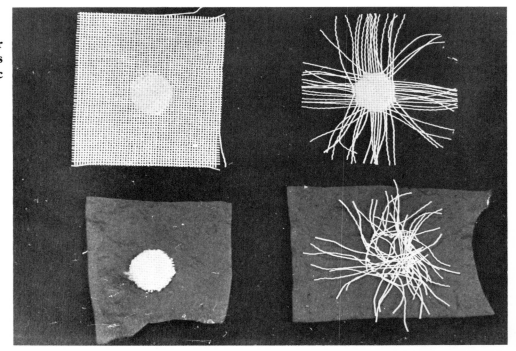

FIGURE 175. Steps for appliquéing canvas to fabric

PADDED APPLIQUÉ

1. Stitch the background with a back covering stitch or use fabric for a background.
2. Stitch the object on mono or penelope canvas. (If an upright, loose, etc., stitch is used, tent-stitch two rows of outline first.)
3. Unravel canvas to the stitching.
4. Pull two threads on each of three sides through one at a time, pointing the needle in.
5. Pull remaining threads through one at a time, pointing the needle in and leaving one area open.
6. Push in cotton padding carefully with a scissors point or crochet hook.
7. Pull remaining threads through one at a time, pointing the needle in.
8. Weave threads through, stitching one at a time or knot in pairs (Figure 176).

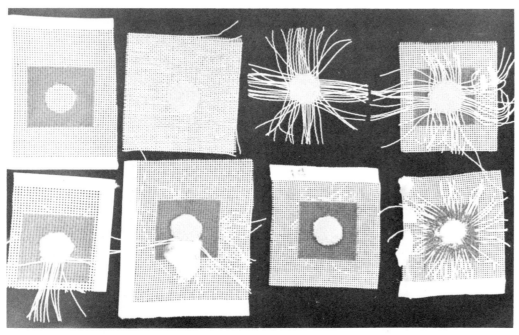

FIGURE 176. **Steps for padded appliqué**

TURN IN—SEWN ON

1. Stitch the background or use fabric.
2. Stitch the object on any type of canvas.
3. Turn the edge under and baste.
4. Sew onto background, using very small invisible stitches and sewing thread.
5. If outline is too rough looking, couch on an outline (Figure 177).

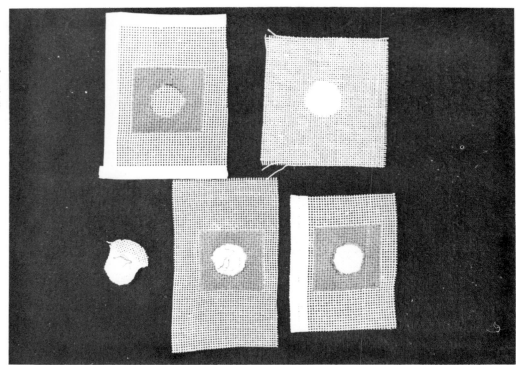

FIGURE 177. Steps for
turn-in–sewn-on
appliqué

FABRIC ONTO CANVAS *(Flat Effect)*

1. Stitch the background.
2. Turn in and baste fabric shape edges if necessary. Felt, for example, does not need to be turned in. The fabric shape can also be outlined with Sobo glue. Allow to dry and cut out in the shape through the glue lines. This will prevent raveling.
3. Pin object flat on canvas.
4. Baste down onto canvas.
5. Sew on using thread and very small invisible stitches (Figure 178).

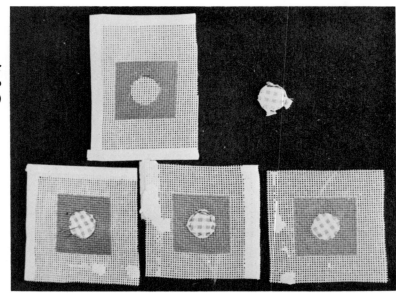

FIGURE 178. Steps for
fabric appliquéd to
canvas (flat effect)

FABRIC TO CANVAS *(Rounded Effect)* *(Figure 179)*

1. Stitch the background.
2. Using the outline of the shape of the object, cut three pieces of felt, one the same size as the object, one slightly smaller, one smaller still.
3. Sew on smallest piece of felt using sewing thread and centering it in the area.
4. Cover with medium piece of felt and stitch, using sewing thread.
5. Cover with largest size felt and stitch, using sewing thread.
6. Turn in and baste fabric shape edges if necessary; or outline fabric shape with Sobo glue, allow to dry, and cut out shape through the glue lines. This will prevent raveling.
7. Sew on fabric shape over felt padding using very small invisible stitches and sewing thread (Figure 180).

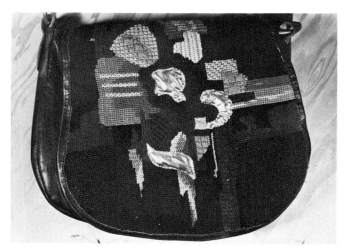

FIGURE 179. Handbag incorporating padded fabric on canvas, by the author

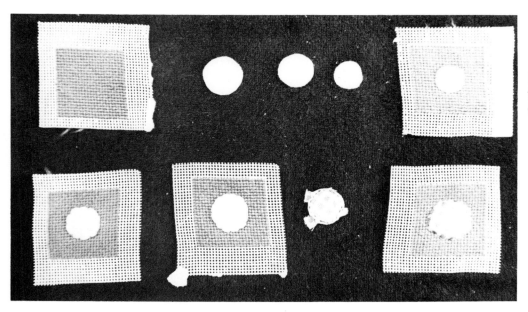

FIGURE 180. Steps for fabric to canvas (rounded effect)

REVERSE APPLIQUÉ *(Figure 181)*

1. Plan layers.
2. Work the layers. Use mono or penelope canvas only.
3. Appliqué the second layer onto the bottom layer using the technique desired.
4. Appliqué these next layers to these two layers and so on (Figure 182).

FIGURE 181. "The Second Day," reverse appliqué design, by the author

FIGURE 182. Steps for reverse appliqué

Appliqué can serve the canvas embroiderer in two ways: It allows dimension to be added by raising an area up, and it affords the embroiderer the ease of adding very small details in areas without having to use fine meshed canvas for an entire piece.

EXERCISES

1. Design and stitch a piece of canvas embroidery employing one of the techniques of appliquéing canvas to canvas.
2. Design and stitch a piece of canvas embroidery that is appliquéd to fabric.
3. Design and stitch a piece of canvas embroidery that employs fabric appliquéd to the canvas.
4. Design and stitch a piece of canvas embroidery based on the technique of reverse appliqué. (Books on molas can serve as a good source of information for this.)

Stones, Beads, and Found Objects

FIGURE 183. Design incorporating seed beads, tree bark, sea shell, and wood beads, by the author

Canvas embroidery can be varied by the addition of stones and beads as well as any number of the vast variety of objects available to us. Such objects should be used with discretion and should be an integral part of the design. They add impact and should be employed with restraint (Figure 183).

SEWING ON

Many jewel-type stones and shells have either man-made or natural holes (Figure 184). If the jewel is transparent, stitch underneath it. The steps are:

FIGURE 184. "Jeweled Butterflies," design incorporating sewn-on jewels, by the author

1. Trace the object onto the canvas.
2. Outline it in tent stitch.
3. Sew the object on with a desired thread as in the illustration so it does not move.
4. Stitch background to the tent-stitch outline (Figure 185).

FIGURE 185. Steps for sewing on jewels

SETTING

Objects do not always provide their own holes, and some do not lend themselves to having holes drilled. In this case the stone is set into a stitched case. Do not use heavy thread for this procedure. If the stone is transparent, stitch beneath it. The steps are:

1. Trace around the object on canvas.
2. Backstitch the outline.
3. Build up the sides of the outline using the detached buttonhole as shown.
4. After the second row of buildup, insert the object and stitch one or two more rows, decreasing until the object is held tightly in its case (Figure 186).

FIGURE 186. Steps for setting a stone

NEEDLEWEAVING

Objects may also be attached by employing needleweaving. The warps can be laid in any manner so that the object is held firmly in place (Figure 187).

FIGURE 187. Warps laid to hold shell and warps needlewoven

COVERING A FOUND OBJECT

Objects such as wooden beads and washers may be attached to canvas and then covered with a thread. The most successful method I have found is to lay an uneven number of warp threads surrounding the object. Then weave around them in the same manner as a spiderweb stitch is executed (Figure 188). These

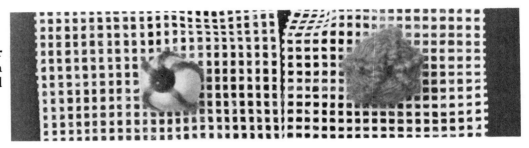

FIGURE 188. Steps for covering a wooden bead

weaving stitches are pushed tightly together until the object is completely covered. Because of the added dimension created with this procedure, it imparts great impact and should be handled discreetly in a design. Flat objects such as washers are best covered with a buttonhole stitch (Figure 189).

FIGURE 189. Washer covered with button-hole stitch

SHISHAS

India has provided the embroidery world with a procedure called shisha work, which is essentially embroidery done with mirrors. However, we should not restrict ourselves to using only mica or mirrors for this procedure but should investigate all types of flat objects such as plastic disks, Mylar, and the like. Traditionally, circles were the basic shapes for this embroidery, but ellipses and free forms may be employed. The basic procedure for attaching them is the same. When the basic tying down is accomplished in shisha work, any number of procedures may be employed for the decorative portion of the stitching. Remember always to pull the tying-down stitches back so the object becomes visible (Figure 190).

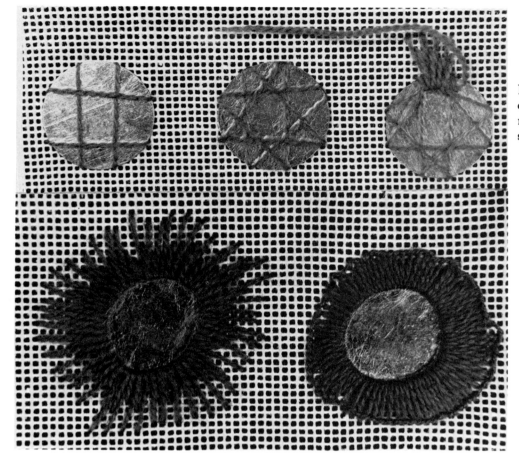

FIGURE 190. Steps for covering a shisha and methods of covering shishas

SEED BEADS

Small seed beads add much to a design and are very easily attached by using sewing thread or embroidery floss (two strands) in the bead color and a beading needle. They are simply continental-stitched into place. When stitching, twist the beads so that they are all angled in the same direction for a uniform appearance. I have found that most seed beads cover 12 or 14 mesh canvas (Figure 191).

FIGURE 191. Attaching seed beads to canvas

When working with objects on canvas, do not get carried away; remember the impact they give, and carefully plan how they are to be used in a design. Nature provides us with a wealth of wonderful objects such as rocks and shells that enhance our canvas embroidery. Different effects can also be obtained by combining objects together—for example, a covered wooden bead on top of a covered washer.

EXERCISES

1. Do samples of attaching various types of objects using each of the methods shown in this chapter.
2. Design and stitch a piece of canvas embroidery employing stones, beads, or found objects.

Attaching Separate Pieces of Canvas

Dimension can be added to a canvas embroidered design by attaching pieces of canvas that stand free on the design. The technique allows areas to stand higher or stand out more than appliquéing canvases allows. From a more traditional point of view, this technique allows you to add wings on butterflies or birds, or petals on flowers or leaves, to name but a few. Care must be taken when using this technique because its impact is great. Careful planning is imperative with all embroidery but especially so with this technique from a strategic point of view (Figure 192).

FIGURE 192. **Separately attached butterfly wing**

I have found that the pieces to be added appear to be handled better if they are worked on interlock canvas.

The steps are as follows:

1. Work the entire background of the canvas embroidery, leaving the area where the canvas is to be attached blank. In order to hold firmly, this area should be at least a half-inch wide.
2. Draw the attached piece on its canvas. Make sure this is drawn so that the canvas meshes line up in the area where the attachment will take place. Attached pieces that are too large will flop about, so keep the size of the attached canvas in mind when designing. Leave an attaching portion on this canvas.
3. Cut the piece out, remembering to include the attaching portion.
4. Edge the piece with a binding or edging stitch such as binding stitching, plaiting stitch, or buttonhole. Do not edge the area used for attaching; edge only that portion that will hang free (Figure 193).

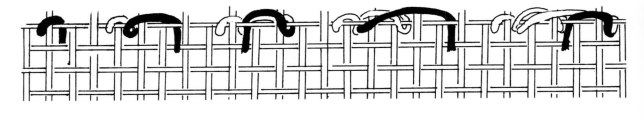
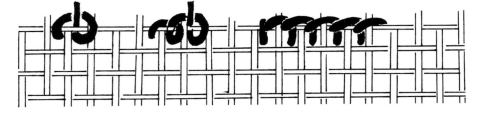

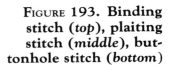
FIGURE 193. **Binding stitch** (*top*), **plaiting stitch** (*middle*), **buttonhole stitch** (*bottom*)

5. Stitch the rest of the attached piece in the desired stitches and design. Care must be taken with the reverse side so that it is neat. Many stitches are reversible, such as the leaf stitch, and using these gives a better appearance. However, stitches that cover the back well are needed for this technique. Do not stitch the attaching portion of the piece.

6. Fold the attaching portion of the piece at a right angle and place this portion into the background canvas, lining up the meshes.
7. Stab-stitch through both canvases with straight horizontal stitches along this fold.
8. Stitch the blank portion through both canvases. A roughly textured stitch works best here to hide the double thickness of the canvas. Any of the texture-rated 6 stitches, such as twisted knot or surrey, work well (Figure 194).

FIGURE 194. **Steps for attaching separate pieces of canvas**

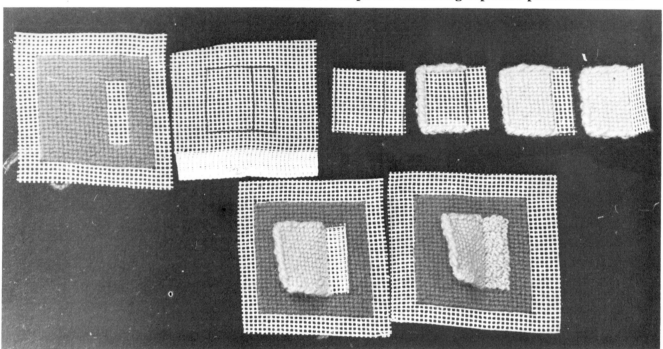

When using this technique, I have found that blocking the background canvas before attaching the separate piece works well. The attaching procedure also is more comfortably worked on a frame.

Do not limit yourself to attaching pieces of canvas on only one edge. Experimentation still shows that strips of canvas can be attached at two edges (Figure 195), or cavelike effects can be achieved by attaching on three sides.

EXERCISE

Design and stitch a piece of canvas embroidery that employs the technique of attaching separate pieces of canvas.

FIGURE 195. **Strip of canvas attached at two edges**

Holes

Canvas embroidery can achieve interesting effects when holes are employed. This technique, however, provides great impact with very negative spaces. It should therefore be used quite carefully. Keep in mind that the holes cannot be very large because there will not be enough tension left to support the remaining canvas. Conversely, holes that are too small present problems of edging.

We have two methods of making holes in canvas embroidery: unweaving canvas threads to obtain holes, and cutting out the holes.

The first method, unweaving, I have found to be the more successful. This method works best using mono or penelope canvas. The steps are:

1. Stitch to the outline of the area to be removed.
2. Starting at the center, snip the canvas threads one at a time horizontally and vertically.
3. Unweave the canvas threads.
4. Weave the canvas threads into the background stitching (if the threads are too short to weave, overcast them with sewing thread).
5. Edge the hole area with a desired edging stitch if needed (Figure 196).

FIGURE 196. Steps for obtaining a hole by unweaving canvas

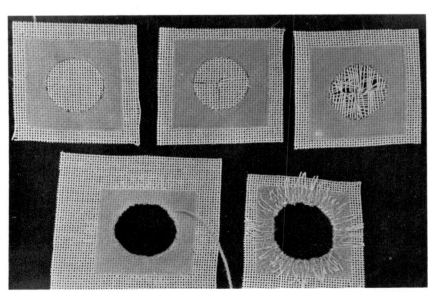

For the second method, any type of canvas may be used; however, I have found interlock easiest to handle. The steps are:

1. Carefully cut the canvas to the edges of the hole outline.
2. Edge the area with a desired edging stitch.
3. Stitch the surrounding areas (Figure 197).

FIGURE 197. **Steps for obtaining a hole by cutting canvas**

Edging stitches are rather limited. Heavy threads are difficult to handle on the edges. The most successful I have found are the binding stitch and the buttonhole stitch. Other edging stitches can be investigated and experimented with. Always try a hole and edging on a scrap piece of the same type of canvas and fiber as the piece you are working.

As with all canvas embroidery, planning is of utmost importance. The impact of the hole is of course crucial, but so is what appears through the hole. Some holes can reveal a variety of fabrics or leathers or more embroidery. Keep in mind that the edges of holes in canvas cast shadows. Finally, do not limit your holes to a circular shape—experiment with various forms (Figure 198).

FIGURE 198. **"Soap Bubbles," canvas embroidered design incorporating holes, by the author**

EXERCISES

1. Do a sample of a hole using the technique of unweaving threads.
2. Do a sample of a hole using the technique of cutting.
3. Design and stitch a piece of canvas embroidery incorporating holes.

Metal Threads

Through the ages one of the most luxurious techniques employed in the world of embroidery is metal thread work or gold work. Even today one is awe-struck by the beauty of these materials on fabrics. Because canvas is a fabric, we can employ these techniques in our work. The basis for metal thread work is the effect achieved when light hits the work, and so when we work this must be of prime importance (Figure 199).

FIGURE 199. "Serpents," design incorporating metal threads on canvas, by the author

We have two methods of working with metal threads on canvas: passing (stitching or sewing the material) and traditional metal thread techniques.

Our first concern with the method of passing metal threads is the materials. Many crochet and knitting metallics are available, as well as those designed for needlepoint, and they work well. Many of these are made of synthetic fibers and do not tarnish. The varieties include lamé, camelot, spotlight, and cloisonné. In addition to gold and silver, metallics are also available in colors, although the range is not great. When working with these threads, take care that they do not unravel, that they cover the canvas, and that they fit comfortably through the eye of the needle.

I usually thread my tapestry needle with a short length and then knot it at both ends. These knots should be pulled tight so they will pass through the canvas holes easily. The stitches employed can be as varied as you desire. However, experimenting with the thread and stitches on a doodle cloth will enable you to see what effects you will get (Figure 200). Many of the techniques previously investigated—that is, needleweaving, drawn fabric (make sure a fine strong thread like schur or lamé is used), or bargellos (Figure 201)—can employ metal threads. These passing threads are best worked on a frame, using stab stitching.

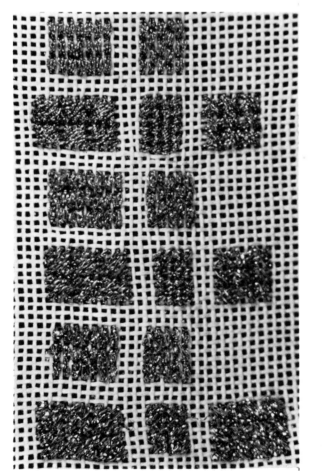

FIGURE 200. **Stitching on canvas with cloisonné**

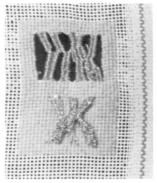
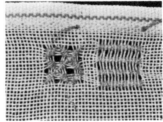
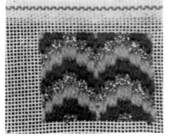

FIGURE 201 (*top to bottom*). **Needleweaving, drawn fabrics, and bargello employing metal threads**

The basis for traditional metal thread work has been couching, and the variety of materials is extensive. The most common couching material used is jap gold. It comes in various weights and sizes and is available in pure silver, pure aluminum, and pure copper as well. Needless to say, these materials are very expensive, and I have found that many Lurex synthetic braids, trimmings, and the like, that are available in the sewing stores, work as well and do not tarnish. In some cases they are even easier to handle (Figure 202).

FIGURE 202. **Materials for metal threads.** *Left to right:* **jap gold (fine), jap gold (medium), Lurex (medium), crinkle, braid, silver, gold lamé (single), gold lamé (double), flat braid, cloisonné, camelot, tube braid, decorative braid, gold middy braid, flat gold, woven gold binding, blue lamé, brown lamé**

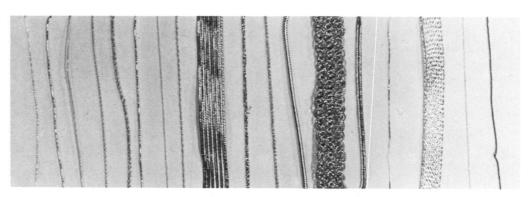

Couching can be employed to cover the canvas entirely or as an accent here and there. How it is used will determine whether it will rest on top of background stitching or directly on the canvas covering it. I usually work with metal threads last when completing an embroidery. Because of the nature of couching, many effects can be achieved. It can be done in straight lines and tied down with a metallic sewing thread (Talon makes one in gold and silver) or with silk sewing thread, Maltese silk, or embroidery floss, or whatever effect you desire. I even use linens and wools for this work (Figure 203). Silk threads

FIGURE 203. **Couching various metal threads**

work best run through beeswax before stitching. Beeswax does darken the color, however. These tying-down stitches can be used in color to produce shading (called *or nué* or Italian shading), patterns, and so on (Figure 204). Curves can also be employed for interesting effects (Figure 205). When couching, always lay your metal thread on top of the canvas, leaving 1½ inches at the end, and proceed to couch for the desired length and have 1½ inches at the other end and cut. Now plunge the ends to the back of the canvas, using a large chenille needle (Figure 206). These ends must be pulled through one at a time. The ends are then attached to the stitching on the reverse side of the canvas by using overcast stitches and sewing thread, stitching to the background stitches (Figure 207).

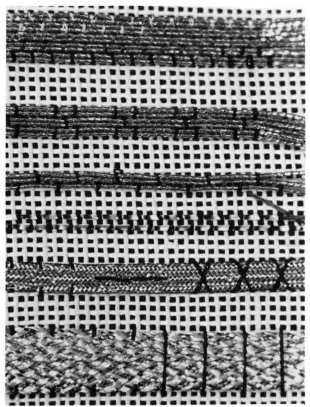

FIGURE 204. Couching using colored threads on metal threads

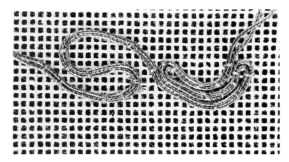

FIGURE 205. Jap gold couched in curves and shapes

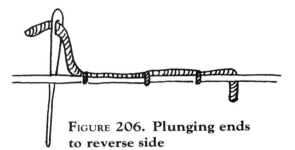

FIGURE 206. Plunging ends to reverse side

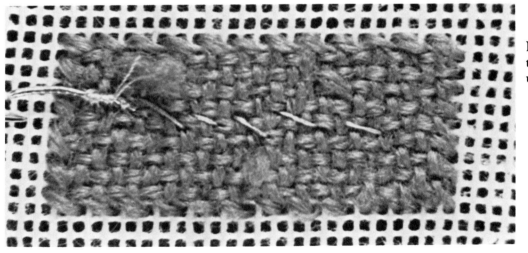

FIGURE 207. Overcast the ends to the back using sewing thread.

The types of threads used for passing can also be used for couching, just as we would couch any yarn.

Couching can also be done over various types of padding. String is a delight to use because of the various weights available, from very fine to clothesline weight. I find the best string is that which has been coated; it is available in sporting goods and hardware stores. It is often labeled "polished." The simplest arrangement is to lay parallel lines of string and couch between them. These strings are sewn down and then the metal threads are couched over (Figure 208). Here again, experiment to find the endless possibilities.

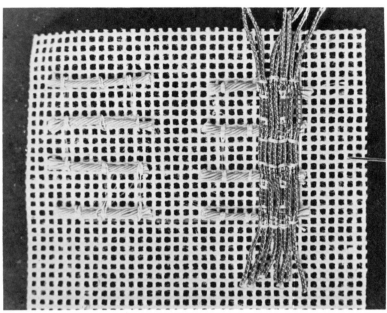

FIGURE 208. **Attaching string in parallel lines** (*left*) **and couching over string**

Many books on metal thread embroidery show couching done over small pieces of cardboard to produce lovely effects. However, cardboard will not stand up very well from a conservation point of view, and I have found that couching over padded shapes of felt or heavy interfacing such as hair canvas or Pellon is just as effective. It is tacked into place with sewing threads and then the metallics are couched on top, leaving the shape uncouched (Figure 209).

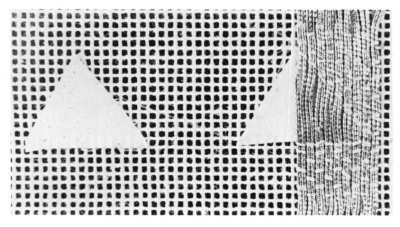

FIGURE 209. **Attaching Pellon shape and couching over shape**

Two very common materials used in metal thread work are purls and bullions. These are actually tiny springs of finely coiled wires. They come in a vast variety and sizes: rough, smooth, bright, and more (Figure 210). A very fine needle is used to attach purl by sewing through the tunnel created by the coil end to end. Silk or sewing thread is used because it does not show. The purl can also be bent into curves. Purl lengths are best cut by resting the purl on a piece of felt that is on a hard surface (you might cover a small board with felt) and cutting the desired length with sharp scissors. This prevents the purl lengths from flying around as they are cut. Purl can also be couched. Experiment with effects to see what results.

FIGURE 210. **Various types of purls and bullions**

Metal threads in the past have also been combined with silk embroidery (commonly known as silk and metal thread embroidery or silk and gold work). As we discussed earlier in our investigation of yarns and crewel embroidery, the techniques may be combined on canvas. I have found, however, that filo silk is the most difficult of the silks to employ in canvas work; it works best on top of a stitched background or on a very fine meshed canvas. It does not lend itself to passing, as matte silk does.

Because of the nature of metallic threads and materials, their impact is great. Also take into account how a piece is going to be used before employing metal threads. On a footstool or piano bench, for instance, metal work is not practical.

EXERCISES

1. Collect metal threads and materials. Label each with manufacturer and content, and note whether they can be used for passing or traditional methods.
2. Do samples of stitches on canvas using passing methods.
3. Do samples of needleweaving using metallic threads.
4. Do samples of drawn fabric using metallic threads.
5. Do samples of Italian shading.
6. Do samples of bargellos containing metal threads.
7. Do samples of various types of couching—straight lines, curves, shapes, covering and not covering canvas.
8. Do samples of couching over strings in various weights and patterns.
9. Do samples of couching over card.
10. Do samples of couching over felt padding.
11. Do samples of attaching purls and bullions.
12. Do a stitched canvas embroidery design incorporating metal threads.

Stumpwork

One of the more popular forms of embroidery produced by English craftsmen in the mid- to late 1600s was stumpwork. The essence of stumpwork was that portions of it were raised, to obtain a high-relief effect. The subjects employed in these historical pieces were usually biblical scenes or pastoral scenes containing people and animals on highly decorated boxes (or caskets, as they were called), frames, or book covers. The techniques used were quite varied, including appliqué of canvas and stitching over padded surfaces and shapes and even over wooden shapes, but the main portions of the designs were usually worked on separate pieces of fabric or very fine canvas gauze and then attached. Embellishments such as beads, jewels, stones, and various types of fabric trimmings were also employed.

Canvas as a textile opens endless possibilities for us to apply stumpwork techniques to our designs (Figure 211). The most important phase of this technique is planning. All the techniques previously discussed are applicable to

FIGURE 211. "The Third Day," canvas stumpwork design, by the author

158

stumpwork, and it becomes a question of how they are to be employed. Here again, planning is of utmost importance. Keep in mind that the very nature of the height of the stumpwork areas will cause shadows within your embroidery. These areas have high impact, and the shadows can affect the color relationships of the piece. I find that listing the order in which objects are to be attached is a big help. Needless to say, the flat background is always stitched first and blocked before the attaching procedures are done.

Padding the background is one of the stumpwork techniques frequently used. There are many methods of accomplishing it. Layers of felt can be built up using the small, medium, and large shape procedure. Once the felt is in place it can be covered with fabric or covered with stitching, using the great variety available such as weaving or satin (Figure 212). Padding can also be accomplished by tacking cotton batting down on the background in the shape desired, covering it with muslin, and finally covering this with fabric or stitching (Figure 213).

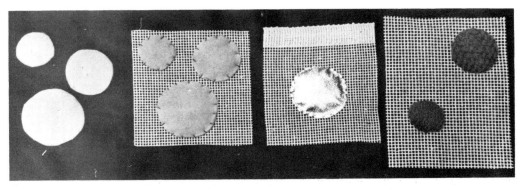

FIGURE 212. **Steps for padding with felt**

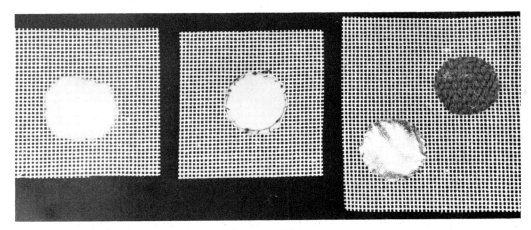

FIGURE 213. **Steps for padding with cotton batting**

Appliqué, which we have already covered, also works very well.

Stitches can also provide the relief effects desired. Some stitches, such as raised buttonhole, spiderwebs, bullion knots, raised cup, and raised closed herringbone (Figure 214) can provide the needed dimension by themselves.

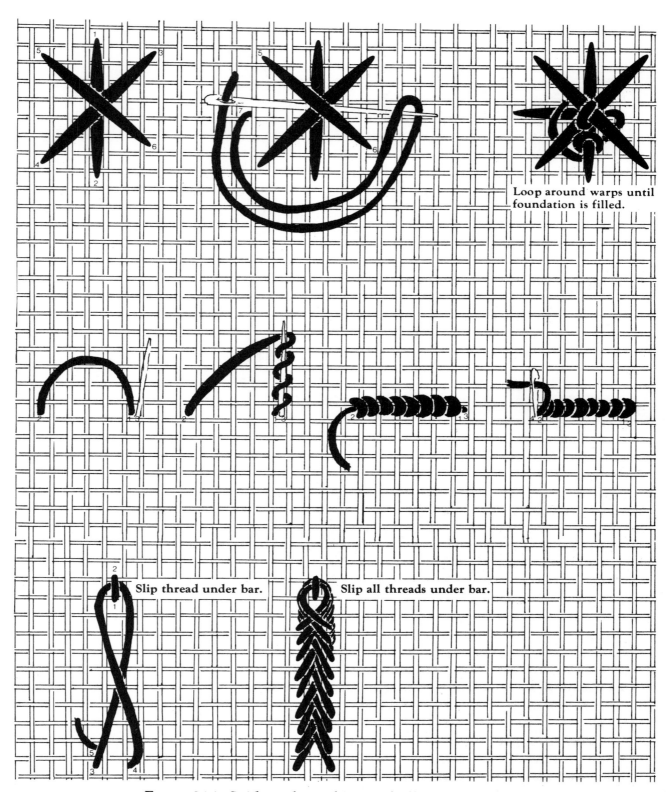

Loop around warps until foundation is filled.

Slip thread under bar.

Slip all threads under bar.

FIGURE 214. **Spiderweb stitch** (*top*), **bullion knot stitch** (*middle*), **raised closed herringbone stitch** (*bottom*).

Stitches can also be built up by layering them, as with the padded satin and padded raised buttonhole (Figure 215), to mention just two. Detached stitches such as buttonhole filling can be done in the shape very tightly and stuffed with cotton batting (Figure 216).

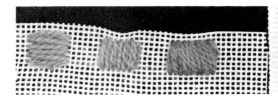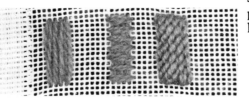

FIGURE 215. Padded satin stitch and padded raised buttonhole stitch

Found objects also can be covered, combined, and attached, as we have done here with the washer and wooden bead (Figure 217).

Stumpwork can also be done by attaching separate units, which can be done as shown earlier. Another procedure is to stitch the shape on a fabric on both sides, sew the two sides together, turn it right side out, and then run wire through to the shape (Figure 218). These are then attached to the background to form a free-standing area.

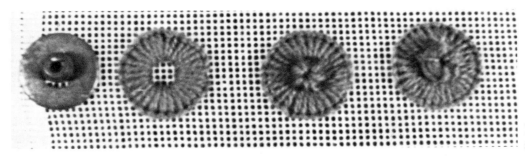

FIGURE 216. Buttonhole filling stitch stuffed with cotton batting

FIGURE 217. Washer and wooden bead covered with buttonhole and weaving

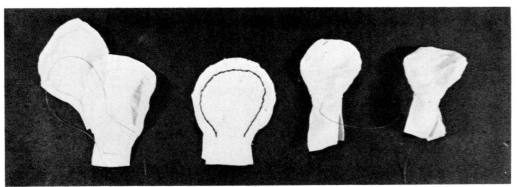

FIGURE 218. Steps for modeling shapes with wire

Separate units can be covered with fabric or stitching and then attached. For this procedure I prefer to use heavy Pellon or hair canvas as the foundation. The steps are:

1. Cut out the shape from hair canvas or Pellon.
2. Put on attaching strings with carpet warp.
3. Apply padding.
4. Cover padding with fabric or stitching.

5. Pull the attaching strings through the background in place and tie in square knots on the reverse side (Figure 219).

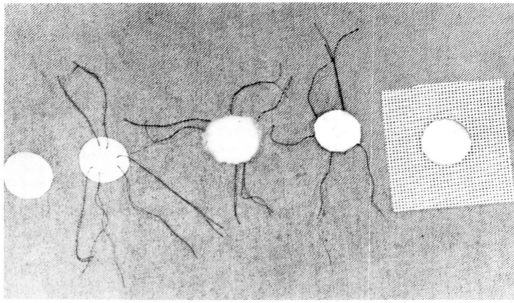

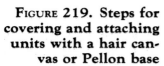
FIGURE 219. Steps for covering and attaching units with a hair canvas or Pellon base

While the traditional designs and objects are lovely, stumpwork designs should reflect our lives and interests today, so experiment with this technique.

EXERCISES

1. Do samples of padding using felt underneath both stitches and fabric.
2. Do samples of padding using cotton batting covered with muslin, using both stitches and fabric.
3. Do samples of raised stitches using crewel stitches.
4. Do samples of stitches that have been built up by layering.
5. Do samples of stuffed areas covered with detached stitches.
6. Do samples of combining found objects.
7. Do samples of separate units attached using both fabrics and stitching on hair canvas or Pellon.
8. Do samples of free-standing attachments such as butterfly wing, flower petal, etc.
9. Design and stitch in canvas embroidery a piece of stumpwork based on traditional designs.
10. Design and stitch in canvas embroidery a piece of stumpwork based on abstract design.

Conservation, Restoration, and Finishing

From the lowly flea market to the elegant auction rooms and antique shops of New York City, purchasers are bidding for and buying needlework both old and new. In fact, needlework both antique and contemporary is not only fashionable but has also become a good investment.

In my travels across the country as an embroidery teacher, I have never been to a class anywhere where the question "How do I clean . . . ?" or "How can I keep . . . ?" hasn't been asked. Women throughout the world today are using needlework, both old and new, purchased and made by themselves, as decorative accessories in homes and offices. The concern for the conservation of needlework is well founded, and unfortunately little reference material is available to the nonmuseum person; so I will give here the basics of the care of needlework. Dirt destroys—as we all know, in this polluted age.

All pieces should be measured before stitching, and the measurements should be noted and kept. The first step to cleaning a piece of needlework either old or new is vacuuming. Old pieces are stitched into a sandwich of coated fiberglass screening and gently vacuumed. New pieces may be vacuumed directly with netting stretched over the vacuum nozzle. This first step applies to all needlework, from quilts and rugs to needlepoint pillows and samplers from 1700.

Needlework (with the exception of Victorian crazy quilts, which can only be vacuumed, and silk pieces, which need professional attention) should be tested for colorfastness. This is done with an eyedropper and distilled water. Using a blotter beneath and blotting from the top, drop distilled water one drop at a time for at least twenty individual drops and blots. This procedure is done for each color and type of yarn or fabric in the piece. If the colors do not run, proceed with the next step. If the colors run, STOP, especially on antique pieces, and consult with a museum as to a reliable conservator to take over. The drop-blot procedure is now repeated just as above but using a mixture of distilled water and Orvus (one teaspoon of Orvus per quart of distilled water). Orvus is a detergent manufactured by Proctor and Gamble that is available at Talas, 104 Fifth Avenue, New York City 10003, or at a good equestrian supply store (it is used to clean show horses). At this point you can be fairly sure about whether colors will run, so resandwich the piece in fiberglass screening and begin washing.

The sandwiched piece is laid in an enameled tray or sink (a bathtub works well for large work) and the Orvus and distilled water solution is pushed through with a natural uncolored sponge. This solution is at room temperature—heat is never used on needlework. Work gently and never scrub, changing the washing solution frequently. The primary aim of washing is to get the needlework to neutral so it will not be destroyed. Using pH test sticks (available in drugstores), test and wash until a reading of pH7 (neutral) is attained. Then rinse with distilled water, pushing the water through with a sponge. After several rinsings, the drying procedure may begin.

Antique pieces are usually dried in their fiberglass sandwich using hair blowers at the lowest setting. These blowers must be kept constantly moving so that heat does not rest on any one area for more than one second at a time. Antique pieces are usually not blocked, because they are so fragile. New needlework pieces, however, should be blocked to stretch them into shape. This procedure is the same for all embroideries and lace, be it canvas embroidery, crewel, blackwork, drawn fabric, or weaving. A piece of homosote board is covered with unbleached muslin or gingham that has been washed in distilled water to remove all starch and sizing. The needlework is laid on top of the board, pinned with stainless steel rustproof pins, and blocked into shape to the original measurements you noted before stitching. Always block with the right side up. NEVER IRON. Begin blocking by putting pins on the diagonals (a bubble will appear across the area), and continue adding pins until the correct shape is achieved (Figure 220). Now let this dry naturally. It will take three days to a week and a half.

FIGURE 220.
Blocking steps

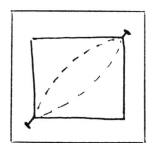 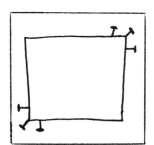 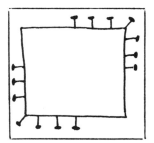 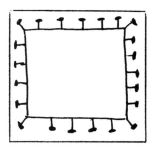

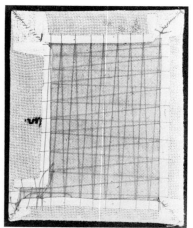

The piece is now ready to be mounted or finished. For those pieces that are to be framed, here are some simple guidelines. Use acid-free mat board or plywood covered with washed muslin as backing. Never let needlework touch raw wood. The piece should be laced on if it is new (Figure 221) or sewn on carefully with pure cotton thread and a curved surgical needle if it is antique. Glass is not recommended, but if it must be used, make sure it does not rest directly on the needlework. A quarter-inch air space is good, and this can be achieved by building up the corners of the frame with acid-free mat board. Pillows can be mounted by the usual sewing methods, but the best filling is polyfill that has been covered with washed muslin. When sewing a pillow,

FIGURE 221. **Lacing**

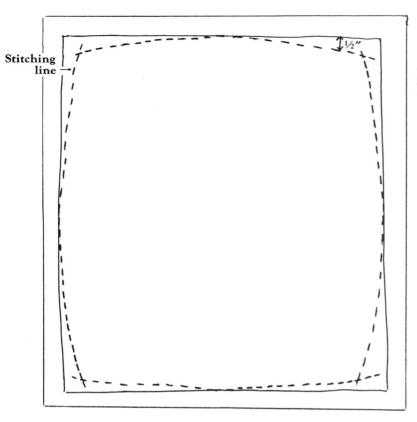

Stitching line →

½"

FIGURE 222.
Pillow stitching

stitch as shown in the diagram to avoid rabbit ears (Figure 222). Never use Plexiglas, which draws dirt around needlework, and do not spray with any chemicals that prevent soiling. Vacuuming with a net over a vacuum nozzle every three weeks will keep your needlework fairly clean, and sponging with Orvus suds once a year will also spruce up your pieces. Orvus does not have to be completely rinsed out, so it is safe.

A word of caution about the hanging and placement of needlework in the home. Light and heat destroy, so they are to be avoided. Areas that receive bright sunlight should be avoided, as should areas over heating units and those with direct artificial lighting. Lighting suppliers now sell bulbs and filters that cause less light destruction. Quilts and large hangings should be lined with a washed muslin so they never directly hit the wall. Velcro mounted across the back and on the wall reduces stress on any one area of a hanging.

Those pieces of needlework that are to be stored should be rolled, not folded, and placed in areas lined with acid-free tissue paper. They should never touch wood or cardboard.

Badly stained white pieces should be soaked in a solution of sodium perborate and distilled water (one teaspoon sodium perborate to one quart distilled water) for a period of several hours to a day and a half. Keep checking to see if the stain has come out, then wash and dry as above. Do not bleach with commercial chemicals or the sun.

Help is available in the form of good advice from a museum with a textile department or the Embroiderers' Guild of America, New York City, or the Valentine Museum, Textile Resource and Research Center, Richmond, Virginia—all of which can direct you to individuals who can help you conserve your embroideries.

History

Canvas embroidery has historically been influenced by tapestry. Tapestry work should not be confused with canvas embroidery. Tapestry is done on an upright loom and woven over vertical threads, thus its history is not included here. True embroidery (of which canvas embroidery is a part) always has a fabric or fiber background. Canvas embroidery is stitchery worked on woven fabric or textile, usually canvas or linen, and the surface is usually completely covered. The history of this form of embroidery serves us as a reference as to what has been done through the ages; history should serve as a stepping-off point; it is not to be copied. In short, history serves the growth of canvas embroidery as an art form.

Here is a brief history by centuries.

THE THIRTEENTH CENTURY

In Germany (Switzerland at that time), counted geometric embroideries were being done on linen with silk. These were mainly used for altar frontals. The Hildesheim Cope of this period used the brick stitch for a background. The brick stitch also appears on many Saxony altar curtains. Although most canvaswork appears to be religious in nature, book bindings were also done in it. Excellent examples may be found in the Victoria and Albert Museum in London (Syon Cope and the Felbrigge Psalter, which is done in silk on a gold metallic background). The ribbon stole found in the Walter Tomb shows the use of a plaited stitch in silk. This era is known as the Opus Anglicanum period. Embroiderers at this time were professionals required to serve an apprenticeship of seven years.

THE FOURTEENTH CENTURY

This century found the uses of canvas embroidery broadening from purely religious work, shown most graphically by the collection of purses and seal bags housed in the Victoria and Albert Museum.

THE FIFTEENTH AND SIXTEENTH CENTURIES

During the fifteenth century, Flanders became the seat of embroidery and the Tudor period was beginning. The sixteenth century found the greatest movement in all forms of embroidery. Around 1560 the greatest output in canvaswork began as the Elizabethan period opened. Work was done in wool and silk, mainly in the tent stitch. Subjects became more varied, as did uses. Objects became more secularly functional, with table carpets, hangings, valances, cushions, and chair seats as the main projects. Work was usually done in all-over patterns on linen canvas 16 to 18 threads to the inch. Nature was the greatest design influence, and often canvaswork pieces were appliquéd to velvet backgrounds. Mary, Queen of Scots, was a notable embroiderer during this period. She worked mainly in tent stitch using herb designs. In this period we also find mention of petit point. Turkey work, done with double strands of wool passed through canvas, knotted, and then clipped to give the appearance of the Oriental carpets that were currently popular, made its appearance. These turkey work pieces were also used for cushions and bench covers and usually were designed in all-over floral patterns. During this period the Italians introduced bargello work. Steel needles were also introduced, replacing the bone needles used previously. Canvaswork projects were usually very large, with many craftsmen working on the same piece. Embroidery was a definite profession, as shown by the fact that the "Broderers' Company" in England was chartered in 1561.

THE SEVENTEENTH CENTURY

During this period the size of finished pieces became smaller and designs simpler. Designs were based on biblical themes with little or no regard for proportion or perspective. The uses of projects became more geared to the home—for example, mirror frames, purses, and pincushions, usually done in tent stitch using silk and wool. As the century progressed, samplers were introduced. These employed such stitches as cross, rococo, Florentine, Hungarian, and eyelet. Oriental styles were also introduced, especially in Holland, where they were extremely popular. The Oriental designs were mainly large florals worked in beautiful shadings with silk highlights. Gros point was also introduced during this time.

THE EIGHTEENTH CENTURY

The Oriental influence was still present, but coarser canvases were being used. Florentine or flame stitch became very popular for larger pieces and was the first popular form of canvaswork in America. Designs began to shift to pastoral scenes such as the "fishing lady" series. All-over patterns became more spread out and pieces were often appliquéd to fabric backgrounds. The lost-canvas technique also became very popular during this period. The quality of work and materials began to decline except in France.

THE NINETEENTH CENTURY

This century produced more variety and less quality. Canvas embroidery became very popular as an upholstery medium. Berlin work was introduced in

Germany in 1835, and these colored designs on graph paper became all the rage. The designs were mainly flowers to be worked in silk with beads and soft wools. This period also marked the introduction of aniline dyes. The French, however, still used traditional methods. Cross stitch and turkey work were very popular, especially with the Berlin work designs. William Morris was the foremost designer at this time (ca. 1860). Machine-made canvaswork was introduced and became quite popular. Penelope canvas was "invented" in France in 1865.

THE TWENTIETH CENTURY

Canvaswork, popular in the twenties and thirties, went into limbo until after World War II, when interest in it was rekindled. The trend during the first half of the century was toward framed works rather than functional ones, although chair seats were often worked. Church work incorporated all forms of canvaswork. The second half of the century brought another revolution, with emphasis on texture effects from stitches. The English have led in regarding canvaswork as a form of fine art and in not restricting their work to traditional methods.

Canvas embroidery has now come into its own as an art form. With the advent of certified teachers, high-quality designs, and, most important, the contemporary embroiderer's thirst for further knowledge, the future of canvas embroidery will be a brilliant part of the history of textiles.

Artists Today

Among the many historical writings about embroidery are frequent references to the meaning of the art to embroiderers of the past. Today's embroiderers, too, are an integral part of the history of embroidery, and their work should be viewed as a statement of our art today. A study of the history of embroidery is not complete unless it includes the work being done in the present.

Included here are a few of the really fine embroidery artists and their statements about their work and the art of embroidery.

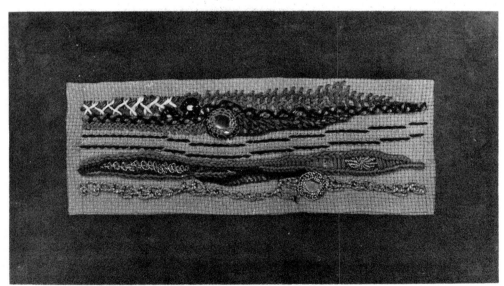

FIGURE 223.

Jo Bucher, Boonton, New Jersey (Figure 223): "Fiber arts have reflected the 'history of the people' throughout civilization. As an active participant in this art form for many years, it gives me great pleasure to see the multifaceted expressions being shared, enjoyed, and appreciated with an increasing awareness."

169

VIRGINIA CARTER, St. Louis, Missouri (Figure 224): "I feel that because there is such a variety of materials and so many learning opportunities available, more people are stitching and working with fiber. This is giving us a more learned public and encourages artists to strive for excellence in both design and technique. Stitchers and fiber artists today are exploring fully new materials and encouraging manufacturers to produce and develop new fibers and textures. Excellence in craftsmanship combined with conscientious exploration of design attitudes and contemporary fibers will make a unique contribution to our art and social history."

FIGURE 224.

ROSEMARY CORNELIUS, Manchester, Connecticut (Figure 225): "I believe that it is not sufficient to be just a good technician. It is the ingenious use of the technique, the stitches, and the materials that contributes to the success of a design."

ANN HARRIS, South Orange, New Jersey (Figure 226): "The fiber arts are related to painting and sculpture insofar as they are a visual art form, but there the similarity ends. Painting with a needle means producing a flat, two-dimensional surface which might indeed be done faster and better with a paintbrush.

"Embroidery, on the level of a fine art, involves textural and spatial elements. These are well expressed through the innovative use of materials and methods combined with traditional stitchery. A wide variety of yarns, threads, string, wire, and findings can be brought into play. The techniques of appliqué, collage, weaving, and cut work may be introduced. Unusual mountings, both free standing and free hanging, may replace the framed picture.

FIGURE 225.
"El Edificio, 1975,"
by Rosemary Cornelius

FIGURE 226. "Red Composition," by Ann Harris

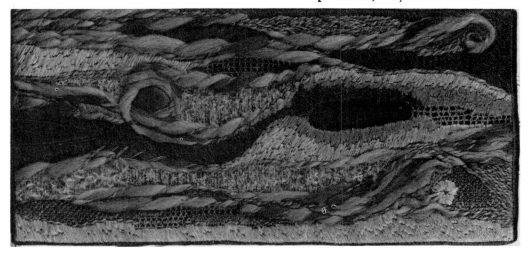

"Imagination and ingenuity combined with a basic knowledge of color and design raise embroidery from a hobby–craft to an autonomous art form."

LISA REHSTEINER, Barcelona, Spain (Figure 227): "The work I am developing under the title 'Broderie' consists on the one hand of returning to the source of ornamental weaving (pattern in reliefs on cloth), and on the other hand of locating this research inside more unusual supports, such as the wire nettings. I am thus trying to show the traditional and elementary processes of embroidery, employing unusual and contradictory materials. The change of the usual scale and condition of a small needlepoint with a demonstration as it were put under the microscope suggests another perception of embroidery to the spectator."

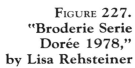

FIGURE 227. "Broderie Serie Dorée 1978," by Lisa Rehsteiner

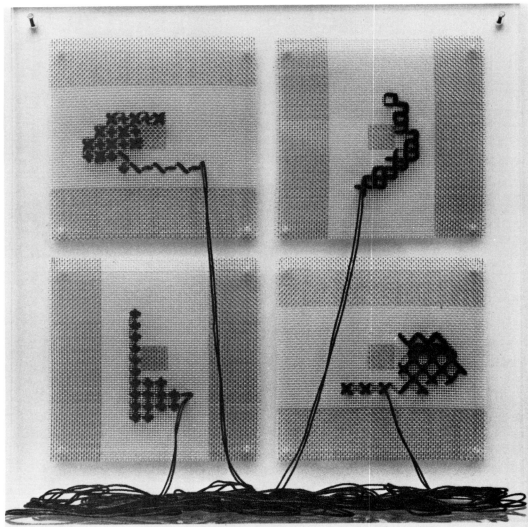

BARBARA SMITH, Glen Ellyn, Illinois (Figure 228): "To embroider means to enhance. I begin with fabric, enriching it with dyes and threads so it takes on new meaning and dimension. When the dye and threads are working together, the color, shapes, enriched, crusty surface, and the image play with one another, interacting, balancing, but never answering all the questions they raise. Edges left off, set askew, shapes unfinished, scenes suggested; the almost-answered question exists. Perhaps it is because I don't claim to know the answers, but more important, I trust to the viewer to supply the answer that is right for him/her."

FIGURE 228.
"Meanderings,"
by Barbara Smith

WILKE SMITH, Albuquerque, New Mexico (Figure 229): "A paradox of stitchery is that a thing it does so well can become a pitfall. Needlework does embellish and enhance exquisitely, and should indeed be used for this purpose. However, its inherent decorative quality too often outweighs its other potentials.

"Subtle or powerful, richly textured and colored, exceptionally dimensional, sensitive to line, shape, and form, stitchery can handle whatever content its creator conceives. Why then does embroidery so often rest lazily on its charm and prettiness alone? In on- and off-loom work, basketry, fabric manipulation, laces, knotting, artists are aware of individual expression, exuberant invention, new combinations of old techniques, original ideas about the very nature of fabric. Yet needleworkers seem reluctant to stray too far from tradition, being happy in the *doing* of the stitch, collecting variations, and with them endlessly repeating the flora, fauna, and geometry, the scale, the very look of the past.

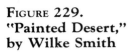

FIGURE 229.
"Painted Desert,"
by Wilke Smith

"When the quality of design and mental/emotional input matches the expertise of the stitching, the medium will again be a major art form. This would seem a worthwhile goal for today's numerous workshops and seminars."

As the author, I would like to add my own statement. You may have noticed that there are no illustrations in the chapter on history. I feel we are working with embroidery today, not in the past. Embroiderers of the past did not dwell on history but rather executed with the needle the images they felt. We must not become slaves to stitches but should make the stitch serve as a tool to be employed to project our images.

Suppliers

The firms listed here fill mail orders.

Anfeis Needlework
19 West Lawn Road
Livingston, NJ 07039

Frederick J. Fawcett, Inc.
129 South Street
Boston, MA 02111

Handwork Tapestries (wholesale only)
P.O. Box 54
Baldwin, Long Island, NY 11510

La Lamé Importers
1170 Broadway
New York, NY 10001

Needle Arts, Inc.
2211 Monroe
Dearborn, MI 48124

Schole-House of the Needle Ltd.
704 By Pass Road (Rt. 60 By Pass)
Williamsburg, VA 23185

School Products
1201 Broadway
New York, NY 10001

Talas
104 Fifth Avenue
New York, NY 10011

Tinsel Trading
47 West 38th Street
New York, NY 10018

United Stamped Linens (wholesale only)
319 Grand Street
New York, NY 10002

Walbead, Inc.
38 West 37th Street
New York, NY 10018